The Cube

. . . Keep the Secret

Annie Gottlieb and
Slobodan D. Pešić

HarperSanFrancisco
A Division of HarperCollins*Publishers*

For Big Jacques.

■ A TREE CLAUSE BOOK

HarperSanFrancisco and the authors, in association with The Basic Foundation, a not-for-profit organization whose primary mission is reforestation, will facilitate the planting of two trees for every one tree used in the manufacture of this book.

FIRST EDITION

Library of Congress Cataloging-in-Publication Data

Gottlieb, Annie.
The cube : keep the secret / Annie Gottlieb and Slobodan
Pešić. — 1st ed.
p.   cm.
ISBN 0–06–251266–8 (pbk.)
1. Self-perception.   2. Individuality.   3. Self-actualization
(Psychology)   I. Pešić, Slobodan.   II. Title.
BF697.5.S43G67 1995
158—dc20

95-4174
CIP

❖RRD(C) 10 9

Introduction

The Cube
is an imagination game—
and more.

In the summer of 1991,
playing it was suddenly the rage
in the coffeehouses of Eastern Europe.
Where had it come from?
No one knows.

Some think The Cube may be
an ancient Sufi teaching riddle.
Lost for centuries, it reappears
in times and places where the soul most needs
to know itself.

Now, it is here.

The warning
on page 17 of this book
protects the power of The Cube—
like a genie in a bottle.
If you open it at the right time,
you will receive rich gifts
of insight and surprise.

But open it too soon,
and the power flies away.

For maximum fun and enlightenment,
do not read past page 17
until you have played the game!
Do not reveal the secret
to those who have not yet played the game!

Part One

The Cube

The Desert

Imagine a desert landscape.

It is utterly simple.

A horizon line.

Sand. Sky.

The Cube

In this desert landscape,
there is a cube.

See it. Describe it.

What size is it?
Where is it?
What is it made of?

(There are no rules, no right or wrong answers.
Describe the cube *you* see.)

The Ladder

Now:

In this landscape, as well as the cube,
there is also a ladder.

Describe it: its size,
              position,
              what it's made of.

The Horse

Now:

In this desert there is also a horse.

Describe it.

What kind of horse is it?
What size? What color?
Where is it relative to the cube and the ladder?
What is it doing?

The Storm

Now:

Somewhere in this landscape
is a storm.

Describe it.

Where is it?
What kind of storm is it?
How does it affect—or not affect—
the cube, the ladder, and the horse?

The Flowers

Finally, in this desert are flowers.

Describe them.

How many are there?
What kind? What color?
Where are they in relation to
the cube, the ladder, the horse, the storm?

You have created a mysterious image:

five elements, arranged in space
in a way that is unique to you.

No one else sees what you do.

Close your eyes and look at it once more.

Now open your eyes . . . and turn the page.

You are ready to learn the secret of The Cube.

Part Two

The Secret

BEWARE
Do not read past
this page
until you've played
THE CUBE

The cube is you.

The ladder is your friends.

The horse is your lover.

The storm is trouble.

The flowers are children.

Stop!

Before you read another word,
ponder what you've just read.

How does it seem exactly true?
And how does it puzzle you?

In the pages ahead, you'll learn
from the pooled experience of those
who've played The Cube before.
But to draw wisdom from this store,
you have to bring your own gifts.

Only when you have thoroughly explored
your desert landscape alone
are you ready to turn the page
and join the community of The Cube.

The Cube Is You

We don't know why,
but we know it's true:
"Describe the cube" seems to be
an ancient key
for unlocking the soul.
You didn't wonder what your cube looked like—
you knew.

In your cube
you have created a self-portrait
of amazing precision and subtlety.
Its size,
its place in earth and sky,
and what it's made of,
all reflect, as in a soul mirror,
how you see
       and feel
       and place yourself.

Look at your cube again.
You'll probably feel a shock
of recognition and revelation,
of simultaneous familiarity and surprise.
Your cube can tell you things about yourself
you didn't know you knew.

Your cube reflects your absolute individuality.

No two cubes are alike!
To prove it, try the game with three good friends.
You will be amazed
by the variety—and the accuracy.

Here is just a small sampling
of the cubes we've seen
in over three years of playing the game:

- black aluminum, 6 feet on a side
- sponge, 1 inch on a side
- scratchproof, shatterproof glass, 20' by 20' by 20'
- an ice cube
- a city-block-sized cube with four different sides and a dark interior

- a fist-sized diamond radiating light
- a cube of cheese, bigger than the moon
- a plump, puffy cube of quilted cotton
- a blue supercomputer
- dark blue ocean water, 2 inches on a side
- a glass house, rocks and waterfalls inside
- a Lucite cube balanced on one point
- solid steel, big as half a house, floating
- dice, in every size (including fuzzy)
- Rubik's cube, in every size
- frozen pink lemonade, 2' by 2' by 2'
- aluminum siding, windows, people living inside
- a desert tent of gauzy, billowing curtains
- a paper cube
- a cube overgrown with grass
- a cube of cloud
- a cube of light

You don't need a psychologist
to explain your cube to you.
In fact—like your dreams—only you
can truly understand it.
It is a message
from you to yourself,

one that unfolds and unfolds,
revealing more each time you look at it.
Months from now, it will suddenly
show you something new.

Here are some hints and questions to guide you
deeper into the mysteries of your cube —
and of yourself.

WHAT SIZE IS IT?

Though we know a six-foot man
whose cube is 6' by 6' by 6',
your cube's size may have nothing to do
with your physical size.

> A huge, powerful ex-boxer
> has a surprisingly small cube — but it's made
> of super-tough titanium, and towed
> by a Blackbird, an incredibly fast,
> sleek spy plane.
> (Before he was twenty, this man survived
> and escaped a Soviet prison camp.)

It would be easy to say
that the size of your cube
measures your sense of your own importance.
But that, too,
would be far too simple.

Your cube could be tiny, yet be made
of gold or diamond—or contain
the secret of life.

> A Canadian housewife
> and mother of three
> saw her cube as a modest little die
> sitting on the sand—
> but on top was the number one!
> (Dice also suggest
> risk-taking and luck.)

Size can sometimes be
a brilliant disguise—or a bluff.

> A short, cocky,
> but warm-hearted cop
> saw a cube so big it filled the whole horizon,

but it was made of nothing more
than the ripples of a heat mirage—
quite literally, "hot air"!

An artist from the former Yugoslavia
burst out laughing, because her cube—
small, sand-colored,
half-buried in the sand—
so accurately portrayed her style
of keeping a low profile
to live her life undisturbed.

You could say
that the smaller a child,
the bigger its cube.

As a baby, your self filled the world.

Growing up was a long,
often painful process
of discovering there's a big world out there
and negotiating your place in it.

The size of your cube
tells a complex truth
about the outcome of those negotiations.

There is no "right size,"
only an infinite variety
of proportions and perspectives.

A large cube
may signal a substantial ego
or a multiplicity of interests:
You include a lot of the world.

Or it may signify
introspection:
a strong interest in yourself
as an object of study
or a realm to explore.

A very small cube could mean
a focus on what is close to you,
or an extroverted interest
in the world "out there";

you may feel small and lost in it—
or that you are its best-kept secret!

A medium-sized cube might declare
an acceptance of being average
or simply a comfort with your place in the world—
a feeling that size is not an issue
and that more important
is "what you're made of."

WHAT IS IT MADE OF?

The material of your cube
is the most evocative,
sensuous,
and revealing part of your self-portrait.

Its surface is your soul's skin,
inviting the world in
or keeping it out.

- Is your cube transparently clear,
translucent (light glows softly through),
or opaque?

- Is it hard or soft?
    shiny or matte?
    fragile or tough?
    porous or airtight?

- Does its surface reflect?
  (*What* does it reflect?)

- What color(s) is it?
  Does the color change?

- Are all four sides the same?
- Are the inside and outside
  the same material or different?

Your cube's core
is how you feel inside:

- solid or open?
- dense or airy?
- dark or light?
- firm or yielding?
- familiar or unknown?

Meditating on the material of your cube can tell you

how visible,
how touchable,
how breakable you are,
and more.

(Glass seeks to be seen through.
Grass and cotton ask to be touched.
Solid rock or steel savors its own weight.
Brick may want to be lived in.
Diamond dazzles with light.)

Is the material of your cube

- natural or manufactured?
- high-tech or handcrafted?
- permanent or perishable?
- common or rare?

Can it melt,
dent,
scratch,
shatter,
bounce,

absorb,
stretch,
leak?

What does this say about you?

WHERE IS IT?

Your cube's placement
in the desert—
relative to sand and sky,
horizon and foreground—
also tells much about you.

- Are you down-to-earth, in touch with daily realities?
- Are you "dug in"? Confidently or defensively?
- Are you deep-rooted? In a rut? In a depression?
- Or on a rise? "Above it all"?
- Feet on the ground, do you reach into the sky?
- Do you float in a realm of ideas or dreams?

Like handwriting analysts and astrologers,
we can "read" your cube's position
in terms of three "zones":

Above the horizon represents
the realm of mind and spirit or
ambition and aspiration.

The horizon line or the surface of the sand
stands for tangible, practical reality.

Below the horizon or below the sand
represents the unconscious, earthy, and instinctual;
family, tradition, and your past.

How close your cube is
to the front of the scene
may indicate how close you feel to others,
how close you let them come,
how much   space   and   solitude   you need.

Or it may suggest
a focus on the immediate—
the near, the now—
or on your long-range visions
of the future (or the past).

Remember—only *you* can interpret your cube!

What does it say to *you* if your cube is
balanced on one point?
"on edge"?
slowly turning?
rolling?
spinning?
heavy, yet suspended in the air?
buried in the sand?
held in your hand?

(More tools for interpreting your cube can be found in
The Vocubulary on page 176.)

The Ladder Is Your Friends

Here is the most mysterious
symbol in the game.

It's not so hard to see
why your cube is you
(or the horse your lover),
but your friends—a ladder?

One thing's for sure:
This game reveals and honors
friends' true importance:
second only to you,
before even your partner.

In the desert dawn
the ladder is alone with the cube,
supporting it, leaning on it,
or simply hanging out with it,
helping to reach its inmost heart,
its topmost height—or beyond,
connecting it to earth or sky—

or letting it down,
standing too far off,
lying down on the job.

This image
tells us another secret
about friends:

The ladder
is a spiritual symbol.

In Jacob's dream
it joined earth and heaven:

>And he dreamed, and behold a ladder
>set up on the earth, and the top of it
>reached to heaven. And behold
>the angels of God
>ascending and descending on it.

>(Are our friends guardian angels?)

A ladder
in Jerusalem's Church of the Holy Sepulcher

stands for Christ's compassionate climb
down into flesh, and his return
home to the Spirit.

Buddhists, as their souls evolve,
mount a rainbow ladder
with seven sacred rungs,
each one a different color.

So any ladder—
galvanized, weatherbeaten, splashed with paint,
even lying on the ground—
is secretly a spiritual
as well as a practical aid.

A ladder is a ladder,
even if it's not being climbed.

Friendship's hidden purpose
is to take you higher,
to help you rise in realms
both outer and inner—
but also to guide you down to earth
if you're a dreamer.

Which way do your friendships point?
How high do they lead?
Where are you going?
Are your friends helping you get there?

> A man at work in the cutthroat world
> of Hollywood agenting
> saw a blackened, twisted ladder
> bent back into the sand.

> "I have no friends here," he confirmed.
> "I've learned I can't rely on
> or trust anyone —
> only my family and myself."

How long is your ladder?
How many rungs?
Do you have lots of friends,
or a few close ones?

> One man's fire-engine ladder
> has infinite extensions,
> reaching to the heavens.
> (He's got friends for *days*.
> And yes, they've saved his life.)

His wife's ladder
is smooth, simple wood
with three or four strong rungs—
her closest friends.

Is your ladder taller than your cube?
Do you look up to your friends,
or they to you?
Or are you equals?

Is the ladder stable,
                sturdy,
                        shaky?

Is it built into the cube's side,
or within its heart and center?

Propped against it,
standing by it,
lying on the ground,
floating upright or recumbent,
stuck independently in the sand,
plunging toward the center of the earth,
vanishing into the sky?

Is your ladder made of

>bolted iron,
>smooth or weathered wood,
>tough, flexible rope,
>cleverly jointed aluminum?

What does its material
tell you about your friends?

>If it's really nothing like your friends,
>consider this possibility:
>the ladder may occasionally be
>your family of origin—
>the ladder of generations.

>One woman's ladder, wrapped in string
>and soaked with water from the storm,
>leaned on her so heavily
>it crashed into her mirrored cube.
>She frowned: "My friends don't do that to me."

>But her mother does.

His wooden ladder, lying down,
had one half-missing, rotted rung.
Not only had his brother died
in an auto accident,
he had lost a friend to suicide.

"It's the kind of old wood ladder
that hangs on the garage wall,
and only your grandfather
knows how to take it down
and run it up to the roof
to rescue your lost kite,"
said one man, with such warmth
that either his old friends are "family"
or his grandfather was his best friend.

Is the ladder made
of the same stuff as the cube?
If not, how do they differ?

A woman whose cube is cloud
has a ladder of sparkling sand
connecting it to the ground.

Her friends may be down-to-earth,
but they're not dull.

A jazz pianist, a Cancer,
has a ladder of water,
lending his friendships the fluidity
of improvisation.

(His wife says
he makes you swim upstream
to reach him.)

Of all five elements, you'll find
that long after the rest seem plain,
the ladder never quite
gives up its enigma.

It continues to puzzle and fascinate.

Friendship, too,
is far more
than meets the eye.

(Turn to The Vocubulary on page 176 for more help
unraveling the riddle of your ladder.)

The Horse Is Your Lover

Now we're on more familiar ground.

Any eleven-year-old girl knows
(in her bones, not in her mind)
that the horse is the promise
of sex: a muscular mystery
moving between her thighs,
an innocent, dangerous wave
of animal power and joy
that comes as itself before
it comes in human disguise.

Your lover is the animal in your life—
embodiment and summoner
of the animal in yourself.

There's more to it
than sex: a lover,
like a horse, can be

       best friend,
       protector,

pet (or pest),
dependent,
renegade,
work horse,
war-horse.

She or he can carry you places
you'd never go alone,

be docile or disciplined,
proud or wild,

run away with you
or from you,
throw you,

hover close,
or just pass by.

The horse is your lover
as *you* see him or her.
You'll recognize its color,
breed, and behavior.

If your horse has a definite gender,
it's not about sexual preference,
but a sign of your lover's qualities
in the language of ancient prejudice:
Is your lover bold, assertive, adventurous?
loved for her steadfast endurance
or for his nurturing gentleness?

If you don't have a lover right now,
the horse is your ideal,

                      or past,

                             or potential lover.

Is your horse a

      Thoroughbred?
      Arabian?
      Wild mustang?
      Pegasus?
      Pony?
      Knight's charger?
      Heavy draft horse?
      Just plain horse?

One man
(whose girlfriend loves to dance)
saw a white Lipizzan.

Another's tall, shy, tawny wife
showed up as a golden unicorn.

The saddest horse
belonged to a lonely man
whose quest through the personal ads
had come up empty.

He saw a wooden sawhorse.

Is your horse

Naked and free?
Saddled or bridled?
In working leather?
Bejeweled and adorned?

(Do you see your lover as

wild?
independent?

domesticated?
dutiful?
magnificent?)

Where is your horse?

On the cube? In the cube?
Running by it?
Circling round it?
Lying down in its shadow?
Standing close,
or far away?

A busy book agent
with a prominent boyfriend
saw her proud horse
way off in the background—
a revealing portrait
of the priorities in her life.

Another woman
(abused as a child,
but healed by her marriage)
jumped from the top of her cube

onto the back of her black stallion,
who carried her inside the cube
where she'd been afraid to go by herself.

A teenager whose intensity
had scared more than one girl away
saw his horse trapped
on top of his cliff-high cube,
screaming to get down.

The interaction between horse and cube
is your relationship as you know it,
in your heart of hearts, to be.
It isn't always what you want to see,
but it's always true—for you.

Your lover may see things quite differently.

You can play The Cube together:
The two of you won't influence each other.
Your vision is yours alone.
That's the magic of the game.

But if you play with your lover,
be prepared for embarrassed laughter
when you come to the horse.

What you each discover
may make you blush with pleasure—
or wince.

One woman,
whose grown kids privately agree
she rules the roost,
sat next to her husband and described
a small, meek horse
huddled under her cube.

Another woman,
her boyfriend by her side,
saw a cartoon horse.
(He *was* kind of funny-looking.)

A veddy logical Brit saw his horse
as a camel. "A *splendid* animal
(after all, we are in the desert!)."
Once he'd learned the secret,
he looked at his wife and shrugged:
"Well, she does have two humps!"

She, a romantic, saw him
as a proud black Arabian
in gem-studded royal trappings.

(He has dark hair
and looks a bit like Prince Charles.)

Another said, "It's a palomino, standing
so far from the cube
there's almost no connection."
Yet this man's dark-haired girlfriend
sat close beside him.
His three blonde daughters ran laughing by,
looking just like their mother—
his ex-wife.

If your horse is nothing like your real-life lover,
        or is far away;

        if your cube merely reflects the horse's passing,
        or you see no horse, no matter how you try;

        if there are two horses, or your horse
        changes in midstream;

        or if your horse is closest to your ladder—

What does that mean?

(For more horse lore, see The Vocubulary on page 176.)

The Storm Is Trouble

You knew that, didn't you?

The storm is a symbol
so classic it's trite.
Think of all those climactic
moments in old movies
when rain pelts the window
and thunder and lightning
punctuate the lovers' quarrel
or the laboring woman's cries.

The surprise
is what this storm brings to light.

Till now, all has been static,
serenely surrealistic.
Only the horse moved,
or rarely, the cube.
The relations between them
seemed fixed and eternal:
your life as a snapshot,
not an action film.

The storm—life's wild card—
throws it all into motion.
The balance is upset.
Suddenly there's danger,
suspense—a plot!

Will the cube be struck by lightning?
Will the ladder go flying?
Will the horse take cover?

As crisis brings out character,
the storm tests you, your friends, and lover:
who protects whom, who is stronger,
how you take "the blows of fate."

Or not.

Many of us
reject the challenge of the storm,
holding it at arm's length—
on the horizon or beyond.
If your storm is small, or out of sight,
your motto is, "No worries, mate!"

This may reflect real good fortune:
You're in a safe and sunny time.

"The storm's behind me,"
the artist said decisively.
She's eight years sober.
Nine years ago a storm-tossed wreck,
drunk and broke down in Key West,
now she's found safe harbor:
her work, a good man, and a gifted daughter.

On the other hand, maybe
you banished the storm
out of stubborn denial:
"That can't happen to *me!*"

Don't knock it.
Denial can sometimes be
the soul's immune system,
locking out bad news,
making its own luck
by sheer force of will.

Yet there are times when
denial can kill.

He smokes two packs a day.
At forty-two, he's been told

he has early-stage emphysema.
He scoffs at his friends' warnings.
His storm, of course, is far away—
brewing deep in his lungs.

Sooner or later,
into every life
the storm will come.
If yours is way far off,
thank God—

and fix your roof!

A storm on the horizon
is a truce with trouble.
You know it's out there,
but at least it's not here,
and things could go on like this indefinitely.

A man of seventy-six, healthy
nine years after bypass surgery,
thought his storm was mortality:
not so far away,
but biding its time.

He kept it in sight
and basked in the sun.

If, on the other hand,
the storm sweeps through—
sandstorm, rain squall, electrical storm—
what do you do?
How do the cube,
the ladder, and the horse
weather it—together or alone?

A woman whose cube
was a gauzy desert tent
took her ladder and her horse inside
to shelter them, while the walls
billowed like ship's sails.
(She's a veterinarian,
romantic and nurturing.)

A man who trusts
his family alone
placed his diamond cube on a hill of sand,
his flowers planted close around.
Round and round them all

cantered the golden unicorn.
Outside her magic circle prowled
the storm, a whirling wall of sand.

Maybe because she's a writer,
one woman lives life as a watcher.
Her horse nimbly dodged
a vicious black tornado
and her ladder spun
head over heels,
while her cube of brushed steel
merely reflected it all.

A warm-hearted young mother,
inclined toward fun and pleasure,
saw her cube as a resort, complete
with palm trees, bar, and pool.
She saw a sandstorm rampage
through this oasis, wreaking damage.
Then everything shook off the sand,
and the flowers sprang up again.
Like a child, she's easily upset—
and then she gets right over it.

The cube tends to survive
the storm in good repair—
unless you've been through hell
in the last couple of years.

    After a marriage that dried up
    (no lovemaking for eighteen months)
    and a bad divorce,
    one man's cube *leaked*.
    The storm left its bottom
    flooded with water—
    unshed tears
    or dammed-up lust?

    A woman, twenty-four years old,
    is struggling to decide
    whether to break up with a lover
    she feels isn't standing by her side:
    "There's thunder, lightning, rain.
    The horse runs away.
    The cube . . . *sinks*."
    Only her weathered ladder stays,
    horizontally hovering overhead—

a sheltering parent
or older friend.

Strapped for cash at sixty-eight,
he had to sell his business
and give up being his own boss.
"The storm is here," he said.
"Strong wind."
And his cube, a gambler's die?
"Gone. It's blown away."

"The storm demolishes everything,"
said an older woman with certainty,
sweeping her hands in front of her.
"It totally changes the landscape."
(Her ladder had been
"dead branches tied together,
lying on the ground.
It has nothing to do with the cube.")
Told the secret, she said,
"Of course. I survived the Holocaust."
Her friends and family had been lost.

Whether the ladder stands fast,
gets thrown for a loop

or knocked flat
reveals the "balance of trouble"
between you and your friends.

Do they stand by you?
Lean on you?
Hover over you?
Have you shared similar weather?
Who's been through more
or taken it harder?

Your horse's behavior
in the storm
may be all too familiar—
and so may your treatment of him or her.

> "The horse is going totally crazy!"
> "Losing its way."
> "It's hiding under the cube."
> "The horse is lying down till it passes."
> "Flying right over the storm!"
> "Are you kidding? It's running away!"

One side of a woman's cube
was wavy strips of mirror

that multiplied the lightning
and scared her horse.

(She believes in facing trouble
but admits to a touch of melodrama.
Her husband, a problem-avoider,
has often accused her
of blowing things out of proportion
and making them worse.)

Short of true disaster,
the storm isn't all bad.
Rough weather
at least brings us together,
brings out hard truths
and hidden strengths
we didn't know we had,
and brings the desert rain.

A woman saw her storm
as one black cloud
poised above her cube,
shooting lightning bolts.
She said her private pain

had proved enlightening
and sparked her growth.

Another woman's marriage
ended in turbulent divorce,
leaving her forty and childless.
Her sandstorm's force
completely buried
her mirrored cube
under a soft-curved dune.

Two red flowers
sprouted in triumph
from its top.

(For more storm warnings, consult The Vocubulary on
page 176.)

The Flowers Are Children

That flowers come after the storm
is no news to any woman who's borne
one child or more.
                              Kids are the reward
for survival,
                    roses at the curtain call,
life's irrepressible renewal—
and ultimate risk.
Their flesh is fresh
as flower petals—
and just as fragile.

"I am responsible
for my rose," said St. Exupéry's
Little Prince.

That's how parents
describe their flowers:
delight in their beauty
in the same breath
with caretaking duty.

People who have children
(or who want them)
usually put their flowers
inside the cube, or close to it,
in the shelter of its walls,
safe from the storm.

A romantic veterinarian
has two young adopted daughters.
She placed a vase of vivid flowers
inside her cubic desert tent.

A reggae musician
(who plans to have two children)
saw two long-stemmed red roses growing
in the shade of his green cube.

A doctor/suburban mother's cube
had daisies round its base,
on a green lawn, protected by
a neat white picket fence.

Sometimes the horse
is appointed protector:

You see your partner
as shield or source.

> More than one father
> has draped his flowers
> in a wreath around the horse's neck—
> awarding them to their mother
> as adornment and prize
> in the Run for the Roses
> we call life.

> To one man's laughing dismay,
> he saw the horse
> peeing on his flowers!
> "Gee, does that mean
> 'Piss on the kids?'"
> On the contrary,
> in the loony logic of dreams,
> she's watering them with her body,
> nourishing their life.

> A woman's flowers grew right
> under her horse—winged, white
> Pegasus, poised in mid-leap.

Her husband's cube indeed
held his flowers close —
but to him, it was *she*,
the circling unicorn,
who wove a zone of calm
and held the storm at bay.

This protectiveness can persist
after children are grown,
especially if parents help with money
or the kids still live at home.

He's retired. His cube is a house.
Two flowers are in a vase
in an upstairs window.
Of his six grown kids, two
are especially close.
They come home every chance they get.
He's never really let them go.

She'd like her two highly gifted,
twenty-something boys
to get on their own feet, already.
But one still lives at home,

and neither is making money.
Her flowers, luminous pink,
glow in the dark
inside her cube
as they hang from the high ceiling,
(de-pending),
upside down.

Some parents plant their flowers in
a small oasis all their own,
a tended garden patch or glade—
or float them in a lily pond.

And some see cactus flowers,
bright as flame,
brought up through a thousand thorns,
the beauty worth the pain.

One survivor of divorce,
the mother of a son,
said the rider of her horse
was killed by lightning in the storm.

The flowers sprang from his grave.

By contrast, people with no kids
(and no urgent wish to have them)
tend to see flowers growing wild,
outside, all over the place.

Nonparents cheerfully assume
the flowers will survive the storm
without the help of horse or cube.

Their flowers tend to be generic,
all of a kind, while parents'
are assorted and specific,
seen in more detail.

Some childless people
love and notice kids.
Some don't have the chance.
And some couldn't care less.

> "I'd like my flowers to be big and purple—
> but they're not," said a poet
> (who rarely meets a child).
> "They're wildflowers, yellow and white,
> very small, hardly there."

A loving aunt, however,
saw a field of brilliant daffodils!

"I *hate* children," said a book agent—
yet the sunflower
between her cube and ladder
was growing vigorously,
spiraling toward the sky.
"It must be my clients."

Your flowers may not always be
children of the flesh.

You'll know if they're budding projects,
ideas, patients, or your pets—

whatever you nurture
that returns the favor
and makes your desert bloom afresh.

(A few more hints about flowers can be found in The
Vocubulary on page 176.)

The Desert Is the World

We never wondered
what the desert meant
till someone asked us:
We'd assumed it was
chosen for its unobtrusiveness—
no more than a blank page
on which to draw your cube.

But then we began to notice
how differently
people portray the desert, too.

To some, it's a forbidding place,
bleak, unnourishing, and harsh.
If anything at all grows there,
it's cactuses.

> (An eight-year-old fighting cancer
> saw a cactus spitting fire
> at his toy-box cube,
> which opened and spat back water!)

Some see the desert's bareness
as an aid to efficiency,
independence, clarity,
or spiritual awareness.

And to others,
it's hospitable and lush.
Say "desert" and they go, "Oasis!"
Their dunes are sensuous,
and they'll often add a graceful palm
for the ladder to lean against
or to give the flowers shade.

One woman saw the desert sand as a beach.

And an actress equipped her desert
with an Astrodome,
so that she could safely watch
the fireworks of the storm.

The desert is the world, of course,
as it appears to you:
your life's bare stage,
a fierce Sahara you can't change,

or a California you arrange
into a comfortable home.
Cactuses
are prickly adversaries,
mirages
alluring illusions.
Oases show the way
to springs of luck and love.

Part Three

Making The Cube Work for You

Now you can see why,
more than just a game,
The Cube is a divining pool—
a mystic tool
for fathoming and changing your life.

Self-knowledge is power.
Only when you gaze
straight at your own truth
can you love it,
> laugh at it,
> forgive it,
> improve it,
> move it,
> and finally,
> fully live it.

The Cube doesn't lie,
and it doesn't judge.
What you see
is what you've got—
and it's more than you thought.

Surprised by the artistry, humor, and wisdom
with which your cube was swiftly drawn?

Meet your imagination.
Each of us has one,
living its own mysterious life
deep within.
The Cube speaks its language
and calls it forth
whether or not you thought of yourself
as an imaginative person.

The Cube is a magic telephone
to this marvelous ally
in yourself and those you love.

Here are some ways
to call on The Cube's power
for insight and guidance—
alone and together.

Knowing Yourself

First, one simple but important fact:
Nobody hates their cube.

If someone said, "Describe yourself,"
you'd list the things you like
and all the things you don't.
But your cube
has no good or bad qualities . . .
just qualities.
And every quality—

> hardness, softness,
> bigness, littleness,
> clarity, mystery,
> brilliance, camouflage—

has its own beauty,
its own survival strategy,
makes its own kind of sense.

Your cube takes you outside
the habit of judging

yourself
and its twin, the habit
of falsifying yourself—
thinking you're other
than what you are.

Though it comes from within,
your cube is objective.
Its reflection of you
is simply factual—
neither flattering nor cruel.

      "Yes, I'm hard,
      yet I reflect softly,"
      acknowledged a woman
      whose cube was brushed steel.
      "People are drawn
      to their own image in me.
      I don't show what's inside:
      I'm dense to the core."

      She was amazed
      by a friend's transparency.
      This woman's cube
      was a glass greenhouse,

with all its inner life
going on in plain view.
It was true:
this friend talked openly
of her most private feelings —
and walked around
her apartment nude!

Can you say
which is the better way to be?
The question doesn't arise.
The Cube shifts your focus
away from comparison
to uniqueness.
Even "transparency" or "hardness"
mean different things
in different cubes.
And each trait's strength
is one with its weakness —
advantage
is limitation, too.

List the most striking
qualities of your cube.
How is each quality

an asset or advantage?
How does it limit you?

After playing The Cube,
you appreciate yourself more:
in *each* trait of your cube
is something to admire.

> (It's a good game to play
> with a roomful of schoolchildren,
> using just the cube.
> *Before* revealing the secret,
> write down what's practical,
> fun, or beautiful
> about each child's cube.
> Then tell them:
> "That's *you*!"
> and let them keep the list
> for when they're feeling down.)

You'll find that you view your limitations—
seen in material form—
with a certain wry affection,
as part of who you are.

"My cube's black marble,
thirty miles on a side —
and I'm looking *down* on it!"
a film director from East Europe
laughingly admits.
"My huge storm is dwarfed by it."

He knows his monumental ego
overwhelms some people.
(He can be tyrannical
on the set.)

He also knows he'd never
have survived in his country
or his business without it.

Sometimes, though, your cube reveals
a trait you'd like to change —
one that's been abstract or vague,
but now you *see* it,
clear and plain:
it has color, texture,
weight, a name.

"I hadn't realized,"
said the woman whose cube was steel,
"how closed I had become.
It's true, I don't let people in.
I don't show what I feel."

Even a cube of granite
isn't written in stone,
but in imagination—
a place where transformations happen.

A trait you clearly envision
becomes one you can consciously work on.

Changing Yourself

Your cube is not you
forever,
as you always have been
and always will be.
It's you *now*.

And the whole vision
of five elements
is your life now.

Five years ago,
your cube, ladder, horse, storm, and flowers
would have been somewhat different.
Five years from now, too,
they wouldn't be the same.
There might be major differences among
the cube you'd see in youth,
in mid-life, and in age.

You do change.
And therefore, you can change.

Like everything you do,
playing The Cube
has already changed you
by giving you a new view
of yourself.
Scientists know
that the observer
alters the experiment.
And alchemists know
that working with certain images
stirs the very depths of life.
By setting synchronistic
forces in motion,
The Cube can work
in quite mysterious ways.

Her simple, well-proportioned ladder
of smooth-sanded wood
floated some distance
from her cube.
"I have good taste in friends," she thought,
"but they don't really touch me."
The next day,
two friends called
that she hadn't heard from in months.

The simplest way
to work with The Cube consciously
is simply to take
its message to heart.

> Aware that she'd fallen into the habit
> of keeping her thoughts and feelings
> to herself,
> the woman whose cube is steel
> now makes a conscious effort
> to show and tell.

> The man with the blasted,
> useless ladder
> bent back into the sand
> resolved to remember
> that he'd had real friends
> before life in Hollywood
> made him so bitter,
> and that some of his oldest friends
> still were.

Another way is to imagine
what it would be like

to change your cube's material
in the way you'd like.

Important note:
You can't just switch
from steel to glass,
or cloud to grass.
You can't turn into someone else.
You have to work with what's given.
Respect your material's nature.
Think what it would respond to.

What would soften steel?
(Heat of passion!
The core would grow molten
and erupt by itself.)

If openness verges
on exhibitionism,
how could a glass house be given
the option of privacy,
of not *always* living
life on display?
(Curtains!)

That's what's missing from your life.
Now you know
what to open yourself to,
or what to bring in.

"The only trouble with this game
is,
you can only play it once,"
a friend of ours said shrewdly.

That's true.
If you knew the cube was you,
you couldn't create it.
It would come from your ego,
not your soul.
And now that you do know,
you've lost your innocence.
You can only speculate, never really know,
what your cube might be
ten years from now.
And any attempt to change your cube
(say, by visualization),
however gentle and well-intentioned,

would be using force
instead of attending to the source.

But remember,
images have
a life of their own.
Trust them.
In your mind's eye,
consult your cube again.

Don't wish,
don't push.

Just look.

Is it the same?
Or has it changed a little?
In the way you hoped?
Or in its own way?

> No, the floating cube of steel
> has not opened up and magically revealed
> its contents.

But it's no longer still.
Its surface now reflects
fast-racing clouds,
and slowly, slowly,
it's begun to turn.

The Cube in Relationships

The Cube's insightful wealth
doesn't stop with yourself.
Playing it with others—
family, colleagues, friends, and lovers—
is, first of all, revealing fun.
It makes you realize afresh
how unique each of us is;
it brightens your awareness of
traits you already know you love;
it lubricates the courtship dance
and hints if new love has a chance;
it gives you a startling deeper view
of people whom you thought you knew,
and—through their ladder or their horse—
shows you how they think of you.

As always, of course,
it's more than just a game.
Any relationship,
once seen in a new light,
can never be the same.

You can demonstrate this in a room
full of people, some of whom
have known each other for ages, some
who are meeting for the first time.
As a party game, The Cube
is a catalyst that can transform
an ordinary gathering
into a strangely memorable evening.

Establish the desert
and go around the room,
inviting each person in turn
to describe the cube out loud. Then ask for ladders. . . .
By the time you reach the storm,
it may seem to be going on too long.
If people get restless
and start chatting about movies, sports, or business,
tell them there are just two more items—
and point out the amazing differences.

As soon as you reveal the secret,
you'll feel the mood change.
Deeper currents are stirred;
a fresh breeze blows through the room.

First come pleased surprise
and embarrassed laughter,
then a new thoughtfulness
as friends and strangers discuss
the appropriateness of their cubes,
and couples compare horses.
Everyone will witness
at least some modest revelations
and forge a subtle bond.
You'll remember those you met
with rare appreciation
and, as a lasting party favor,
take your own new insight home.

––––––––––––

Between close friends,
The Cube becomes
a touchstone of affection,
a private joke,
a diving bell,
an excuse for talk.

"Oh yeah, I forgot how big your cube is!"

"Don't tell me that no-good horse ran off again."

Friends confide,
console each other,
analyze themselves together—
a role more ancient than
therapist or confessor.
The Cube gives to this intimacy
a refreshing new vocabulary.
(Imagine complaining about your ladder
instead of your mother!)
It can show where your friend is sore,
what part of his life is hurting.
Knowing each other so well,
you may each see more
in the other's imagery
and use it, tenderly, to heal.

Occasionally, your ladder will reveal
a harsh truth
about your friends:
that they're not your equals,
that they tend to lean all over you,
that they're shaky and unreliable
or chronically down and out
or going nowhere—
taking you along for the ride.

Now that you know,
it's up to you to decide
what you want to do
about the caliber of your friends—
or if you like them fine
the way they are.
The Cube is just a mirror.

———————

You've just met someone and you're wondering:
Could this go further?
The Cube is—among other things—
a great icebreaker
(seduction tool, say some).
It lets you talk on a level rare
for a first date, and learn more
than you could from discussing movies
or even exchanging life histories.
In fact, you're exchanging life mysteries.

Also, with The Cube
as your heart's radar,
you're not flying quite so blind.
You can get the lay of the land:
a preview of what to watch out for,

what he or she needs in a lover,
an afterimage of loves before,
a sense of whether she or he is more
open or inscrutable,
yielding or immutable.
You'll get a strong whiff
of the person's style,
which tells as much to the soul
as a dog's sense of smell.
Maybe best, you'll get a glimpse
of his or her imagination—
the oddest, dearest part of someone.

Is this what you were seeking?
    A delicious surprise?
        Someone else's cup of tea?
            Or an invitation to catastrophe?

———————

Between lovers, or life partners,
The Cube brings conflicts to the fore,
shows you in no uncertain terms—
in the poignant semaphore of dreams—
what the other is feeling,
brings to light the differences

that may help fill each other's gaps,
yet act as hidden stumbling blocks:

> She's a shameless romantic—
> her whole scene
> straight out of the Arabian Nights.
> Her jeweled steed,
> jet-black and royal,
> is, in his own soul,
> quite practical:
> *his* horse is a camel!
> (Would *you* bring a camel flowers?)
> Secretly, she'd love
> to be coddled, courted, catered to.
> Damn him—
> he admires her strength!

It's so revealing
(rudely shocking, moving, healing)
to see your relationship
through each other's eyes.

> A potter, she's quiet as a nun.
> Her boyfriend is the cocksure one.
> But her cube is huge and calm,

adobe painted white with lime,
and her horse is walking toward it.
His plastic cube is small and clear,
snugged down in the foreground sand.
On the horizon, far and high,
his graceful horse goes running by —
not even glancing at the cube.
Apparently she's more sure
of him than he is of her!

Your lover's horse
not only shows you
where you stand in his or her life
and how she or he perceives you,
but also the Lover your lover seeks —
the role she or he tries to fit you into,
whether or not it really suits you.
Does he see you in harness
when you need to be free?
Does she keep you at a greater distance
than you want to be?
Does he seem to be looking
for a different horse?

Once seen,
it all can be discussed.
Even clashing visions
may not be sufficient reason
to give up in disgust.
The key to change
is not to try to rearrange
and force your worlds to harmonize,
but simply to become aware
of each other's needs and fears.

Playing The Cube makes crystal clear
a truth too easy to forget
in love or in a heated fight:
the world's not only as you see it.

No matter how intense the charge—
or if we love for fifty years—
at our core, we do not merge.
Your lover looks through different eyes,
two worlds existing side by side:
two images, unique and whole,
of the oasis of the soul.

Part Four

Celebrated Cubes

A Portrait Gallery

Willem Dafoe

actor, Platoon, The Last Temptation of Christ, Mississippi Burning

THE CUBE
It's got black lines to it, on each edge, and it's transparent. About two and a half feet square. It feels like, you know, those joke ice cubes that are made out of a very heavy plastic, kind of a molded see-through.

Lucite?

Exactly. It's not quite solid, there seems to be a little air in there. Initially I was looking at it from farther away because I was seeing the larger landscape, but now that I'm describing it I feel that it's right here.

THE LADDER
It's a stepladder, and it's painted yellow, and it's got a little chain across both sides to hold it, to keep it from spreading, rather than a steel thing. It's splattered with paint, and it's quite close to the cube. It's wooden with metal hardware to it.

THE HORSE
It's a brown horse, it's quite far away, it's got white markings on its feet and black mane and black tail. It's very museular. I don't know horses so well, but it's like a wild horse, like a

... mustang. It's running, right along the horizon. It's a weird kind of perspective, visually, because it's running directly along the horizon, but it's not on the horizon, so it's actually quite close, but it's not *near*. Know what I mean?

You're seeing it silhouetted against the sky?

Yeah.

THE STORM

It's quite far away. As I look out it's off to the left. The horse is actually running *toward* the storm. It's dark clouds, and there's a little clearing between the horizon and the clouds, but then they're quite billowous and quite dark, and they pretty much fill . . . I keep seeing this picture that you're describing as if it's in a frame, and they really fill all the way up to the top of the frame.

THE FLOWERS

As I look in the foreground, there's a green, patchy, very poor soil, and little scrubby blades of grass, and then there are little clusters of black-eyed susans. The cube is pretty much center, pretty much center, and halfway—no, about a quarter way into my vision, and then the horse is three times that, and then the storm is way in the back, and on this side the black-eyed susans are quite close to me, like if I turned, I could probably walk twenty feet and pick them.

COMMENTS

This is quite comforting. I think I'm quite healthy, from my description.

> *Well, you're down to earth, clear, outlines . . . boundaries!* [he laughs] *And a joke ice cube only looks cool . . .*

> *[The stepladder may reflect Willem's double life. Besides his film career—and prior to it—he has been a member of the Wooster Group, a New York experimental theater ensemble, for seventeen years, and is married to its director, Elizabeth LeCompte. They have a twelve-year-old son, Jack. So Willem's friends live in two worlds, and the chain joining the two sides of the ladder might portray the flexibility he needs to move back and forth between them.]*

The storm is energy, or . . . ?

> *Trouble, but it has a positive aspect, too; it's energizing, often. Maybe challenge is a good word.*

The horse is running toward the storm, right!

> *Your horse obviously has a life of her own.*

Right.

> *She's not hovering around you . . . she's busy . . . and she's not afraid of challenges.*

That's her. Good interpretation. Good game.

Gloria Steinem

pioneering feminist; author of Revolution from Within

THE CUBE

I feel like it's floating, and you can see through it, even though it's on one of its points. You can see the horizon line through the cube. It's either standing there in the distance, or it's floating—I'm not sure which—not terribly far away, but in the middle distance. Most of it's above the horizon. You can just see the horizon line through the point. I'm not sure that there's any material. It may just be the outline of a cube, like a Magritte painting.

THE LADDER

Somehow it won't be leaning on the cube. It doesn't want to do that, so . . . but it's also not on the ground. It's to the right of the cube, one end resting on the ground, inclining off into the distance slightly. But resting on nothing, as far as I can see. It's a little taller than the cube, but that's also because the cube is a little more distant. The ladder is made of wood, and I think it's green. Kind of an old-fashioned green, like that. [*She points to the marbled, moss-green wall in her apartment.*]

THE HORSE

It seems to be on the other side of the cube. The ladder's over here, the cube, here's the horse, and they're both facing toward the cube. The horse is standing at the side, and it's a kind of palomino color, whitish beige, but it has a very shaggy mane, a little darker, and a very shaggy long tail, not groomed at all. It's just standing, facing the cube, but the cube feels like it's closer to me, and both the ladder and the horse are now a little more distant.

THE STORM

It's rain, not snow, and it's that kind of storm that darkens and pours suddenly and then clears up. It's a lot of rain, but it feels like it doesn't affect those three things. It just comes down.

THE FLOWERS

The flowers are more in the foreground, closer to me than the cube. Though it doesn't make sense, because if I were standing, this wouldn't be true, but nonetheless it seems as if I'm looking over the flowers only by a few inches. It feels as if there are quite a few, but this is the edge of them, so I'm looking over the edge of them to the desert. They're sort of red and purple, like anemones. . . . I don't know how many there are exactly, there could be quite a few, but they're not neat, they're just like a field of flowers. The field is close to me, and I'm sitting in it or standing, looking over to this other vista. They are regular-size flowers, so I can't explain why it is that they're so tall. Maybe I'm sitting down.

COMMENTS

It makes sense to me that I would see myself as transparent in some sense . . . both for positive and negative reasons.

The ladder is definitely not leaning on you! And it's green . . .

It's going up into the sky, it's not on the ground. . . . I wonder what it means that they're not connected, they all have space in between them, though the horse is facing the cube.

Do you have a shaggy lover?! Or have you ever had?

No, and it's strange also that the color of the horse was palomino, because certainly physically, I've always been attracted to dark-haired and sometimes dark-skinned men, but anyway dark, not fair. The horse makes the least sense, but that also may make sense in another way: I'm past the "lover" stage!

Could the flowers be the young people your work has influenced, the young women you said impress you

because they know what you know, as feminists,
though they're less than half your age?

When you said they were things I was nurturing, I just
trusted that, I just believed that. They're the only thing that
is in my immediate vision. And they feel wonderful and
new, or unfamiliar. Like little miracles.

Tim McGraw

country singer/songwriter, Not a Moment Too Soon
(Curb Records); *five awards for best new country artist of* 1994

THE CUBE

It's translucent, it looks like, and has a lot of different sides, feels like a lot of different textures inside it. It's like there's a lot of different cubes and cubicles inside of cubicles in there. And it's translucent, see-through, you could see the background through it, but you can still see the edges of the cubicles everywhere inside.

What's it made of?

I don't know if it's made of anything, really. It's just kinda there.

How big?

Not real big. It doesn't take up a large area of space. I would say seven or eight feet square.

Is it sitting right on the sand?

No, it's up in the air, moving a little bit. Floating.

THE LADDER

A wooden ladder. It's old. To the left of the cube, just layin' there. Four feet long.

THE HORSE

It seems like it's towards me more. Up in the foreground. And it's black. And it's kinda just hangin'. Doing nothing in particular. Just kinda hangin' there, in profile, against the sunset. It seems like it's waiting.

THE STORM

It's off to the left, way in the distance. On the horizon, kind of rolling. The clouds are building up and rolling a little bit. But nothing seems to be bothered by it.

THE FLOWERS

Back toward the clouds, it looks like. Back toward the clouds with the horizon straight ahead of me, with a reddish sun background and the rolling clouds off to the back, way in the distance to the left. And the flowers seem to be in the shadows of the clouds.

COMMENTS

The cube is you. Wow. That's strange.

A floating cube may mean you live in ideas, or in the spiritual world, more than in the practical world.

Well, I know that's true! I'm not practical at all. I can't tell you how to pay a phone bill.

The storm is trouble, and it's far away. The flowers are children.

Troubled children?!

Have you got any children?

Not yet but I've been thinking about flowers a lot lately, 'cause I just bought a new house and there are a lot of places I want to plant flowers. There's like two hundred acres, and yesterday I was out on four-wheelers and I was on this big meadow, and I thought it'd be cool to have this big field filled with flowers down there. Maybe that's why I thought of it. And it was cloudy yesterday.

The flowers can also be creative, children of the mind. When you write songs, do they come from trouble?

Not usually. Not consciously, anyway. I just get in a mood all of a sudden.

·I like it, I like the picture I created. Like a painting. It doesn't seem troubling at all. It seems kinda peaceful, actually. I hope I don't discover something that ain't supposed to be there. . . . I'm just kidding.

Does it fit?

Yeah, it does. Because the cube was definitely the main thing that I thought of, the center, the focus. . . . That's cool. I'm going to try that with my girlfriend.

Jasmine Guy

actress, The Cosby Show, A Different World, Melrose Place

THE CUBE

It's glass, it reflects the sun almost like a mirror, so you can't see inside of it, you don't know if it's solid or not. And it's very hot from the sun, so when you touch it . . . like glass, it absorbs that heat. And it's about . . . I'm not good with measurements, but I can put my arms around it. Let's say it comes up to my chin, and when I hold my arms out I can put my arms, my hands on both sides.

Except that it would be hot.

So you can't touch it.

THE LADDER

It's in the sand, down. Lying on top of the sand. It's old, wooden, weatherbeaten, like I would find it in my grandmother's house.

How far from the cube?

You can see them both in the same picture, but it's not close, you'd have to drag it to the cube. It's not that high, maybe seven feet.

THE HORSE

It's brown. I don't know that much about horses. It's shiny, it has a saddle, it's well groomed. It's waiting, like, for its rider, up on a dune, like a hill, above the cube and the ladder. It's looking to the left. I'm looking at its profile.

THE STORM

It's beyond the dune. It's gray and dusty, like some kind of windstorm. And it's in the direction that I'm going. I'm walking towards it. I see it ahead of me. I'm not sure what kind of storm it is, because I don't know the desert terrain, but it looks gray and it's blowing, it's sandy, and where we are it's clear, as if you were looking ahead at a rainstorm.

THE FLOWERS

The flowers are coming out of the cacti, and they're big, white flowers like gardenias. And some of them have little pink veins in them.

Where are the cacti?

Oh, they're spotted on the periphery of the picture that I see.

COMMENTS

The cube is you.

Oh, my God!

Embraceable—but too hot to handle.

And mirrored, and you can't look inside! Oh, great!

But you said almost *like a mirror. So potentially maybe someone could see inside, if you wanted them to.*

Yes. If someone wanted to.

Your ladder suggests good old friends who are like family to you.

Yes. Absolutely. I was just talking about that. The friends I have in my life have *been* in my life for about a decade. We grew up together. When I left home and they became my friends, they stayed my friends. I don't have . . . I have a *few* new friends, but the people I call on are the old ones.

Ohhh . . . the horse is my *lover?* He's not looking at me! He's waiting. *[shouting]* Come on, gallop on down that hill! *[laughs]* Ohh, man! Oh my goodness! I don't have one, so I'm assuming that he's waiting . . . for me to take care of what I need to do, I guess.

I've had a lot of trouble in the last couple of years with that part of my life. Dating has been very hard for me, as a celebrity, it's just been . . . so much that I've just taken a break now. I want everybody out of my house.

Exactly, so that you can say "I'm falling" and they're there, and you can also say "These are my dreams," even though they may be bigger than most of the people I'm with, and they don't chastise you for your ambition; they don't go, "Well, what else do you want? You're being selfish!" I'm going to continue to work and make money, that will always be an issue. That's something I can't fix.

This horse is very well groomed. He's not a wild horse. And he's patient. He's a stallion. He has muscles, and he's shiny, and he's dark brown. And—he's *there!* It's not like he's galloping away or galloping towards me, he's just sitting there, and this is the *third time* that someone has told me that! My friend who is psychically inclined says, "You already *know* him." That of course bugged me out, 'cause I had to go through everybody I knew, and I'm saying, "Not him, not him, not *him!*" And then a minister told me, "You already know the man, you're just not ready for him. He's waiting for you."

That's exactly what the picture is!

I *know*! That bugged me out when you said that was the man! I think I'm kinda knowing who it is, I'm just rejecting it. I'm like, "Mmm, it can't be him, that's not what I pic-

tured for myself. He's just a friend." But it may be a friend
. . . that I need.

*You're walking right toward the storm. Is that charac-
teristic of you?*

Yeah, I'm always walking right into the middle of storms.
Really. Especially at this time of my life. I've done it several
times, 'cause I'm not afraid. I'm looking for something, and
I don't think I'll find it if I don't walk right into it and see
what it is. Feel it.

After I finished *A Different World,* my vision was
clouded. I didn't know if I wanted to act anymore; I didn't
know what I wanted to do; I didn't have any meaning in my
life; I broke up a five-year relationship, and I knew I was in
for some hell, I just wasn't sure what that hell *was.*

So you started your own production company.

Yeah, because waiting for jobs just wasn't my . . . that's so
uncharacteristic of me. I worked steadily since I was seven-
teen, I was a dancer, I did Broadway, I decided I wanted to
act, I came to L.A. . . . I was used to hustling, and hard work
begets work. I just couldn't passively watch my career drop.
And so at least I feel like I'm trying, and I can look back on it
and go, I did what I knew and had the resources to do. All of
these signs are coming to me that I'm in the right direction.

It's just a matter of time, and there's something I'm supposed to learn that I haven't yet.

The flowers are children. Or they're creative projects.

They're very, very beautiful . . . but they're coming out of those cacti! Some people think cacti are beautiful.

Do you?

Yeah, I have them in my kitchen window. First I bought them because they were the only ones that could withstand the heat from the picture window. The other plants were just cooking. Then I started to appreciate them, and they've survived, and when I go out of town they're still there. Yeah, I love the cacti that blossom. I've always wanted children, that was part of why I broke up with my boyfriend. He didn't want any. He really didn't want them, under any circumstances. And I said, 'Well, where are we going? I've been with you since I was twenty-four, I'm about to turn thirty, I have to find something else.' With all that we had been through, with the love that was so evident to everyone . . . it was sad.

Douglas Coupland

author of Generation X, Life After God, Shampoo Planet

THE CUBE

Well . . . probably like the monolith in 2001, except reproportioned. It became more like a smooth black sugar-cube shape. It's smooth and black and seamless. Black box. It's just sort of as if you put it down on top of the sand. . . . Probably because I just moved, it's about the size of a moving box. They're on my brain at the moment.

THE LADDER

Just a generic household ladder comes to mind, wood. It's the type that if you want to make it longer you can extend it. I don't know what you call those. Extending ladder. So if you want to go to about the third or fourth story, you can do it.

Where is it relative to the cube?

Not right next to each other. They're arranged sort of like sculptures in a Noguchi garden, like stones in a Japanese garden, so if you want, you have to walk a few steps away from them. The ladder's lying on its side, so it looks sort of like a baby crib.

THE HORSE

A horse! . . . I'm not a very horsey person. My dad is, but I'm not. Well . . . I suppose it's brown, with a white patch on the head, and, uh . . .

Hard to see this one?

Yeah, just 'cause what's a horse doing in the desert? . . . Oh! It's found a little bit of grass, and it's eating. Okay.

Where?

Again, it's like rocks in a stone garden. If you can see a picture of one of those Kyoto gardens, these things have been arranged in that sort of placement. You've got the cube, and the ladder, and the horse grazing, in that sort of spatial relationship. It's all very well thought out.

THE STORM

Hmmm . . . It sounds implausible, but there's a waterspout! Have you ever seen waterspouts? They're quite strange. It's literally like a column of water that goes up, and the ocean's flat, but you've got this pillar of water. It's quite magical. I saw it at my cousin's offshore in the Bahamas. Now I've mentally placed myself in amongst the three objects, and the horse is calmly eating, and there's this waterspout, and it's off in the distance, but I don't think it's going . . . It's going to pass by us. But it's creating really nice light. Because there's a little bit of lightning, not much . . . no, suddenly I have to start thinking about the sun, and these clouds that are causing the waterspout are causing a lot of darkness over there, but I guess it's around the end of the day, because we're in that kind of golden light, that magic light you get just before sunset? So I guess it's a storm at the end of the day. But no one's freaking out, because it passes by.

THE FLOWERS

Oh! You know where the flowers are, the flowers are *everywhere!* There's a place in Africa, a place I always wanted to visit. It's called the Nama Valley, and it's where a lot of plants that we . . . well, it's the home of the daisy, basically, and oxalis, and gerbera, and there are trillions, literally trillions of seeds lying dormant in the soil, and then every six or seven years the rain, water comes down from the Congo, and all the flowers germinate and grow at once? And we have millions of square miles of daisies and flowers?

And so suddenly the desert's all making sense now. The storm is like the storm that came and left the water that grew all the flowers, and that was the waterspout, so it's this magnificent piece of almost like psychic architecture? That left the water that allowed the flowers to grow, and so the horse has lots to eat. . . . I'm trying to figure out how the box and the ladder fit in. I always liked the black box in 2001, because you could never get into it. It contains some ineffable mystery that you're not supposed to . . . I guess it holds the promise that in the end, no matter how much you think you know, there's always one greater mystery that lies in wait to be known.

As for the ladder, I don't know. I don't think I've ever used a ladder in my life.

Maybe that's why it's lying down?

I think probably knowing me, if it were sand, I would probably stick it in just to make it a bit more sculpturally interesting. In fact, I would definitely spike it in, just to make it more rock-gardeny. . . . So here we have everything. We have lightning, we have flowers, and the waterspout, and the magic cube—and the cube is mine!! It's not like it's someone else's cube. I feel very proprietary about it. I don't feel proprietary about the ladder. I do feel that's my cube, don't take it away. You can't have it. And the horse is not my horse. It's just there. It's like, Hey, how ya doin'? Great. And the ladder's like, well, someone left a ladder here. And . . . *[softly, like a painter stepping back from a canvas]* There!

Oh, right! I don't even know if I want this, necessarily!

COMMENTS

The cube is you.

Oh! Okay! *[prolonged laughter]* Oh, man, this is scary! . . . What do most people say?

All different things.

Really? Because . . . of *course* the cube is black and contains mystery, and it will be revealed to you only once! People say packing crates or something? That's so funny. I can only think of one—there's only one possible thing that that cube could be. It's not arbitrary. Again, the reason I like it and it has to be *that* cube is because it contains one great mystery that will be revealed eventually. It's not like you're not ever going to find out. It will be revealed, but only at some transformational point in your life. You can't just get it, like buy it, you can't crowbar it open. It will be revealed to you.

The ladder is your friends.

How many types of ladders are there? A ladder is a ladder is a ladder, isn't it? I don't know . . . I think my response is more inert, like . . .

First it was lying down, and then you thought maybe you'd stick it up in the sand.

To make it more interesting. But when I think—Oh, my! *[with real regret]* I'm not nice enough to my *friends!!* No!! Oh no!! . . . Okay. Now what was everything else?

The horse is your lover.

Oh! That's interesting!

Which has an independent existence in your picture. It's friendly, but it's not right next to the cube, and it's not perceived as yours.

Yes! It's like, you're your own . . . And those spatial relationships are not haphazard. There's definitely a thought-out relationship between them. Now what's the storm?

It's trouble, it's challenge, it's life's power to disrupt.

Well, to me it's off in the distance. And the other thing is, whenever something bad happens, I turn lemons into lemonade. The storm is that beautiful light, and flowers, and drama, and again it's architectural: It's like this mystic spike of water.

The flowers are children; or they can be ideas or projects.

It certainly would be, I think. Certainly for the time being, because this year's leitmotif is ideas and projects. Like three million trillion of them. Isn't that funny!

They could be your readers.

I don't know. All I know is that there's just zillions and zillions of them, and they cover everything.

And so what do most people say? I'm just so convinced that everybody would see things exactly the way I saw it. It's hard for me to even believe they wouldn't see . . . I've got three really good friends here tonight. I'm going to do this on them. I can't wait.

Judith Regan

polymedia producer; president and publisher, Regan Books (an imprint of HarperCollins); President of The Regan Company (a division of Fox Broadcasting and 20th Century Fox); editor to Rush Limbaugh, Howard Stern, etc.

THE CUBE

Glowing; bright orange; bright yellow; reflecting from all sides; large; right on the horizon, in the middle, centrally located. Brilliant, perfectly shaped, Oz-like. *[laughs]*

Do you know what it's made of?

It's shiny. Jewel-like.

THE LADDER

The ladder is leaning against the cube on the right-hand side. It is bedecked in emeralds and rubies and diamonds. And it's much higher than the cube. It goes on and on and on, up through the clouds into the sky.

THE HORSE

A white horse, a stallion, long mane, combed, beautiful, running, galloping, healthy.

Near the cube?

In front of and to the left of, running toward.

THE STORM
Thunderstorm, to the left, approaching the cube, dramatic, rainbows, about to happen, expected . . . welcome. Beautiful. Magnificent.

THE FLOWERS
Climbing up the ladder. Intertwined, gorgeous, roses, lilacs, sweet-smelling, all over.

COMMENTS
The cube is me? God . . . does that mean I have a healthy sense of myself? Oz-like . . . *Regan* means "king" in Gaelic.

The horse is my *fantasy* lover! . . . Actually, all my lovers have been beautiful. Physically beautiful. Absolutely! That's why I have beautiful children. I procreated with two beautiful men.

I love the fact that I put all the jewels on the ladder.

You have priceless friends you look up to, who lead you to high places.

I love flowers, too. Flowers are a big part of my life. Look, they're everywhere, all over my office.

The flowers twined around the ladder suggest that you nurture your friends and authors, and/or that your children are your friends.

I have a great relationship with both my children. They're very much my children; I don't view them as my equals in terms of friendship. It's very much parent-child. But we're very, very close, and they're an integral part of my life. Usually I bring them with me when I travel. So the intertwining makes sense.

It's interesting, because the storm . . . There's always a storm. There's always a storm somewhere in the picture. And to me, the storm is as intriguing and beautiful and interesting as all the rest of the picture. Because out of the storms in *my* life have always come the rainbows. So I always view all of that as pretty. It's a challenge that I welcome, and it's consistent with how I've lived my life. In fact, I start my book, which is called *The Art of War for Women*, with an old Chinese story:

> There's a farmer who's very poor, and he has one plow horse. And the horse runs away. And the townspeople come and say, "Oh, this is such bad fortune! This is such bad fortune!" And he says, "How do you know this is bad fortune?" Two weeks

later, the plow horse comes back with fifty other plow horses, and they say, "Oh, this is such good fortune, this is such good fortune!" And he says, "How do you know this is good fortune?" And then his son is riding one of the new plow horses and falls off and breaks both his legs, and they say, "Oh, this is such bad fortune"—and then there's a war, and he can't go to war because he has broken legs!

It goes on and on and on like that—and to me, that's the storm. The storm means water, it means flowers. So I don't view that as dark. I view it as part of the process, as part of the picture. And it's over here, so it's not going to destroy. It's rainbows, there's vitality, there's life. And I have always loved thunderstorms. Mmm, God, I love a good thunderstorm. Love them! Even hurricanes—I love all that! I've even enjoyed the earthquakes I've been in.

Were you in Los Angeles during the January 1994 earthquake?

No, but it's funny, because I went the very next day. I had a meeting with Rupert Murdoch, which was the beginning of this chapter of my life. And it started the day after the earthquake, and I was just about the only one on the plane going in that direction. I went into this dust bowl, with after-shocks! There was one that week that was about 5.6. And everybody said, "Oh, you can't go, you can't," and I said, "Are you kidding? And miss this opportunity?" And *all* of it was an opportunity. Because to me, being in the eye of the storm . . . I don't fear it at all.

Shokei Matsui

World Champion, Kyokushin Full-Contact Karate, 1987; New Kancho *(Director), International Karate Organization Kyokushinkaikan*

(Note: Mas Oyama, world-famous founder of this strongest and most authentic Japanese karate style, died suddenly in April 1994 at the age of 71. His chosen successor, Shokei Matsui, stepped into Oyama's formidable shoes at only 31, bypassing senior karate masters on whose support his success as director will depend. The International Karate Organization Kyokushinkaikan has 12 million students worldwide.)

[translated from the Japanese]

THE CUBE

It's a diamond the size of a pyramid. I was just walking along in the desert, and suddenly I ran into it.

THE LADDER

It's very strong, made from wood and iron. It's leaning against the right side of the cube, slightly taller than the cube. The bottom legs of the ladder are anchored deep in the sand.

THE HORSE

Do I only get to have one? . . . It's white, it stays near the cube, and it's my servant.

THE STORM

It's a big sandstorm, and it's coming straight toward us. But I know it's only going to last one day. And the cube will protect the ladder and the horse.

THE FLOWERS

Fields and fields of flowers behind the cube, as far as the eye can see.

Erica Jong

bestselling author of Fear of Flying, Fear of Fifty, Becoming Light:
Poems New and Selected

THE CUBE

Oh, it's a wooden cube like a child's block, with letters on
the sides of it in red and blue and yellow. It's sitting in the
desert and as I'm approaching it I can't tell what the letters
are, but as I come close to it I see that it's spelling out my
name—E-R-I-C-A—in red, blue, and yellow. Primary colors, but they're sort of worn down, because it's been in the
desert for *centuries*. I don't know how it got there.

   How big?

Big enough to hold in your hand. Like a block, a child's toy,
maybe a foot square. I walk up to it and I'm astonished to
find it there in the desert with my name on it.

THE LADDER

It's sticking out of the sand, but it's leaning up against a
cloud. Which seems like it shouldn't be solid, but it's pretty
solid. The ladder is golden, gleaming, and I'm not sure as
I'm looking at it whether I should climb it, or whether at
the end of the ladder, which is so inviting, could possibly be

the angel of death, the *malech hamovis*. Is it ecstasy, is it death, is it the beginning or the end?

How close is it to the cube?

Nearish.

THE HORSE

It's a white Arabian. It has a beautiful sculptured muzzle and blue eyes. And it's *my* horse. And I think the question is whether I'm going to get on the horse or climb the ladder. The horse has no saddle or bridle or anything, but I'm a good bareback rider. In this dream, anyway.

Where is it relative to the cube?

It's off to the left, facing away, as if it wants to gallop home, but it's waiting and pawing the ground.

THE STORM

It's like a black cloud, but it's not in our immediate vicinity. It's off in the distance. It *might* be coming in our direction, but that's not clear. Maybe it will just float right by without getting us.

Any effect on the other elements?

No . . . except that I'm thinking, as I'm looking at this, that maybe we should make this decision fast *[whether to get on the horse or the ladder]*. Before something happens.

THE FLOWERS
A wreath of red roses around the horse's head. Very beautiful.

COMMENTS
The cube is you? I put my name on it, so I must have intuited that.

> *It's also an alphabet block, so it's letters, the tools of your trade.*

That's right. . . . It's weird that people see the cube in different ways. I can only see it as an alphabet block!

> *What is the golden ladder?*

As I get older, I have fewer and fewer real friends. Fewer and fewer people I would really identify as friends. It used to be, when I was younger, I thought I had many friends. And I've discovered that the number of people who really qualify are few. And they're golden for me. They're precious. Because they're not replaceable. I also think I understand why old people in their eighties or nineties will always tell you at a certain point, "I might as well go now. All my friends are dead." When I was younger I didn't understand that. I think that's part of the association in the dream, that climb to the . . . I think that when you reach a point where your cohorts are gone, and the special ones, the ones who are the witnesses to your life, are gone, you're very much adrift in the world. And then you sort of get ready to leave, to climb that ladder into the clouds. Maybe to rejoin them, above . . . wherever.

The white horse . . . If the horse is a lover, it's interesting that I've got him white, Arabian—sort of dangerous and pure all at once. Because Arabians are very fast, and they are erratic horses, more than Thoroughbreds. They're very fiery horses, and they have very beautiful faces, whereas Thoroughbreds have more plain, puddinglike faces. So there's beauty and danger, but also there's purity, as if a unicorn had wandered into the picture. And I guess what I demand with lovers is for them to be rarer than the unicorn, beyond all human limitation, which of course people aren't. So very often in earlier stages of my life I've broken up relationships because the person was not the unicorn that I was seeking.

Now I understand that everybody is *and* isn't the unicorn. There's a kind of restlessness that throws things away without having explored them. I try not to do that anymore, try to have more patience. You *can* catch the unicorn, but not by demanding absolutes from people. People can become more than they seem, but they have to be given enough leeway.

And that quality has to be allowed to come and go in them.

Right.

Why are the flowers around the horse's head, like a garland? They may be creations, your children of the head. They may not be your daughter, they may be your books, your poems.

It used to seem to me that the work I did proceeded out of an intimate relationship with somebody, as if that person were my muse. And I still tend to use the man I love as my muse, reading him bits of a new book, needing his approval. As if that connection was so essential to the work. It's a recapitulation of the child-parent relationship, of the person-God relationship. I do tend, when I get stuck, to lay stuff out for Ken *[Burrows, her husband]* and then say, "Do you think this works?" And if he likes it, I'm encouraged to go on. So maybe the flowers around the head of the lover is that laying out of creative "roses."

Joe Diffie

country singer and songwriter, Third Rock from the Sun *(Epic)*

THE CUBE

Well, it's black, and it looks like one of those Rubik's cubes. Shiny black, but there are lines through it. It's all shiny like shiny linoleum, black. And it's rather small, and it's just sittin' there. It looks like it's probably in the distance, so it just looks small on the horizon. In my mind, looks like it's about four, five inches tall.

> *But maybe that's because it's far away? And if you got close to it, it might be very big?*

Exactly.

THE LADDER

Ohhh! Well, the first thing comes to my mind is that old movie, with Jimmy Stewart in it? And they had a ladder on an airplane that was crashed in the desert, and they were trying to fix the plane up? I forgot the name of the movie, but . . . it's just sitting on an airplane that's half covered with windblown sand, and the ladder's up on the wing. It had red on the sides, and silver rungs.

It's closer to me than the cube is and to the right. . . . These are the weirdest questions I've ever answered!

THE HORSE

I see a chestnut brown Arabian horse, and it has a saddle on it, but there's no rider. And its tail is stickin' straight out, mane is blowing in the wind. And I see it off to the left at about the same distance, not quite the same distance as the cube. And it's sideways to me.

Facing towards the cube?

Yeah.

THE STORM

It's way past the cube on the horizon on the left-hand side, and it's a dust storm. And it just looks like . . . you see clouds overhead, but you can tell it's just a dust storm.

Not causing any problems?

Right.

THE FLOWERS

Flowers in the desert? I see 'em growing on top of the cube! I don't know what kind they are. They're pink and yellow.

And white. Pretty good-sized. Growin' on top of the cube.

COMMENTS

Oh, really? The cube is me??

You like to wear black?

Uh . . . *yeah!* Wow, that's weird! That's wild. And what else is there, what about me?

You said like Rubik's cube. Does that mean you can turn and twist it? The moving parts, like versatility, being able to adapt, to do a lot of different things . . . do you identify with that?

Absolutely! Absolutely. Jack of all trades, master of . . . only one. The ladder is my friends? Huh. That's wild. Now what does that signify, that I had it next to an airplane?

You tell me.

Well, maybe I relate to that 'cause it involves a team, a bunch of people workin' on this airplane, trying to get it to fly. It takes everybody with different skills, trying to do their part on the airplane to make it fly.

So that's what it's like when you do a record or a tour?

Yeah, exactly. The horse is my lover. Wow. Well, that kind of applies!

Arabians are beautiful.

Real spirited, and beautiful, and—yeah, that applies really well!

Lucky you.

The storm is trouble? Yeah, I want it way away.

The flowers are children.

Well, I have four children. They're thirteen, ten, five, and three.

All at home . . . right on top of the cube!

Absolutely. Well, that's pretty cool! Ask somebody to draw a picture of it.

Katherine Neville

bestselling author of The Eight *and* Calculated Risk

THE CUBE

It's the Ka'ab in Mecca. *Ka'ab* means "cube." I think it's made of stone. It's black, and 120 feet. It's the center of Islam. It's the altar where God asked Abraham to sacrifice his oldest son. The Koran tells the story differently: The oldest son was not Isaac, it was Ishmael. He was the son who was supposed to be sacrificed but who was replaced by a ram. And the black stone at the center was that altar.

Have you ever been to the Ka'ab?

I don't even know if women *can* go there. But I've seen pictures of it. It sits on a big open plain that's kind of sand-colored. And way, way out beyond it, forming a circle, I see a wall with arches supporting it, like an aqueduct. Usually around this time of year it would be very crowded, because next week is Ramadan, but I'm not seeing it that way. I'm seeing it isolated on this plain. I've just come back from Konya, Turkey, a similarly sacred place for the Sufis, and just as we left, everyone was flying off to Mecca. They actually have to circle the Ka'ab seven or eight times. I guess in my vision they're still on the way there.

THE LADDER

I immediately see Jacob's ladder. Angels going up and down it. It goes up to heaven, and it comes down near the cube, and the angels are running up and down. Gabriel: isn't that who Jacob wrestled with? It's really interesting: Ishmael was the founder of the twelve tribes of Islam, and Jacob became Israel, the founder of the twelve tribes of Israel. So in my first two items I've got the entire foundation of the Western world—all but Christianity.

And Jacob had a stone too, for his pillow.

I've got both the stones together. Too bad we can't get the religions together a little bit.

THE HORSE

The White Horse of Prague. It's a magical white horse that founded the city of Prague. The story is that he jumped from the castle wall across a moat, and on the spot where he landed they built the city. I see the White Horse of Prague, jumping in the air, jumping from the wall that surrounds the plain, down toward the place where the ladder comes down beside the cube. He's jumping right to that spot. . . . In October, I went to Prague, because Ivan Havel, the brother of Václav Havel, the Czech president, is a very good friend of ours, and he invited me to Prague to see these standing stones that had recently been discovered, some of the oldest megaliths in Europe. Apparently the Celts were in the area of Bohemia a long time before they got to Spain or England or France. I also visited the place the White Horse leapt from, and I saw a lot of paintings of the White Horse leaping through the air. I didn't know it was a legend. I thought it was true. Everyone there believes it.

THE STORM

The storm over Toledo. A storm moving down the way it does over Toledo. El Greco is a character in one of the books I'm working on. I've been to his house in Toledo, and I've seen the view that he had from the house. And I really relate to El Greco's paintings. No one else could create the colors he created. Whenever I see that painting, *Storm over Toledo*, it always makes me feel good. The strange thing is that Toledo also was founded by a white horse. It jumped from the walls and across the moat of Ferdinand and Isabella's castle. So I suppose Prague and Toledo belong together.

THE FLOWERS

There are pear blossoms on the moat that the horse jumps over, floating on the moat inside the wall. Pear blossoms are very important to me. They smell really good.

The cube is you, so how do you identify with the Ka'ab?

It's hard for me in a way. It's not just feelings, because I have so much knowledge about what a cube means in terms of symbolism. Any cube-shaped space, in the esoteric tradition, symbolizes the altar. And the word *altar* means not just where you sacrifice to and make connections with God, but it also means *alter*, as in change. It's a place where you are transformed. The Ka'ab is a perfect example: They go counterclockwise around the stone at the center, moving through the process of transformation.

So your purpose in life is involved with transformation?

I haven't transformed myself much spiritually since childhood, but the one transformation I have gone through, happening a little more every year until it's out of my control, is the feeling that I'm here to help the world and other humans transform in the direction that we're supposed to. I was told that by other people before I really felt I wanted to accept that as any kind of mission. People who came from Tibet and India and China and other places just said, "We came to see you and to talk to you." I was a banker! I had written *The Eight,* and I had written *Calculated Risk.* After *The Eight* came out, people started to write me letters from all over the world. My book is now in twenty-two countries. I always answer the letters. And I found with quite a few, it didn't matter what country they were from or what age they were—I've had people nine years old and people ninety years old write to me. But some of them seem to know me better than anyone I've grown up around, that I've lived with, or my family, or my closest friends. We had a really strong connection. I'd known I had to write books since I was very young, but I didn't know why. In the past few years, especially since *The Eight* has come out, I've started to realize why, or what exactly I'm supposed to be doing, and so I just let myself do it. So it is a transformational process. And I think that's probably why I imagined myself as the altar.

And why Jacob's ladder?

I do have an acquaintance in Virginia who is a channel for the archangel Gabriel! . . . When I was asked to speak last year at the Ateneo de Madrid, they asked me, "Why did you go from writing this very transcendental magical mysterious book to writing a book about the material world and finance?" I said, "Actually, I wrote them both at the same time!" But now I understand why. People who are highly spiritual just go off on a mountaintop, or disappear into the sky, and I don't think that's appropriate for the world we find ourselves in now. Saying you can't work in a bank or on the stock exchange if you're spiritual is ridiculous. We have to bring spirit back into matter. The friends I've made since my first book came out in 1989 have been people who are moving toward this way of thinking, who really feel it can't be one or the other. The angels are coming *down* to see Jacob! They're not dragging him up into the sky! So I think they're trying to bring him a vision of what he's supposed to be doing.

And they're going both ways, connecting the two realms, so that's a model for us.

When you say the horse is the lover, the person I actually live with, who's my spiritual mate, is the world-famous, seventy-five-year-old brain researcher, Karl Pribram. The town of Pribram is within spitting distance of Prague! And that's where his family came from, though Karl was born in Vienna. When he moved to the United States as a young man, he went to military academy. He was in the horse-drawn artillery, and his job was to train the polo ponies and the dressage horses. And I've always told people as a joke that he was a horse in a former existence. Horses always come up to him and try to kiss him. And so, without knowing that was the lover, I picked a horse that fits with Karl's persona. And he *would* jump off a castle wall to protect me! And be next to me.

And found a city with you?

Neville means "new city," so that was an amazing thing to say!

I have a real affinity for storms. I was told that I was born in a thunderstorm, so when I am in a storm of any kind I feel in my element. Even if I'm depressed or frustrated, I just like the feeling of storms. . . . There have been a lot of storms brewing on my personal horizon lately. I'm hoping those will dissipate.

The pear blossoms? My first best friend, and only best friend, really, as a child, for many years, was a giant pear tree. And developers cut it down. Not just that, but they had to blast it with dynamite to get the roots out, because they were building a new school, a junior high school, that I was going to have to go to. And when I went and looked and counted the rings, the pear tree was almost two hundred years old. And so I was very embittered. And I later became a tree rights activist. . . . Everyplace that I've lived, I've planted pear trees. When I came here, I got these little sticklike twiggy trees from the supermarket, and I put them in the ground in a place where they'd be sheltered. And then I planted flowers around them to attract the bees. Last year my little pear trees got so many pears on them, they almost tipped over! I'm hoping they live through the ice storms this year.

According to our game, those are your children!

My books are my children, and books come from trees! From the beginning of every culture, trees have given us books: the first Teutonic alphabet, the Runes, was carved on twigs. One of the reasons I plant so many trees is that I feel guilty as an author for using so much paper. Not guilty, exactly, but responsible to restore the balance.... So I've been saving my trees from ice storms, tying them up. And I've been protecting my books from other kinds of storms for the last year.

Karl Pribram

brain researcher; Professor Emeritus, Psychology and Psychiatry, Stanford University; Director, BRAINS (Brain Research and Informational Sciences), Radford University; recipient, National Institutes of Health Lifetime Research Career Award

THE CUBE

It'd be transparent. Quite large. Since it's an imaginary cube, it'd be, oh, I'd say the size of about six houses. Really large.

Do you know if it's made of glass?

Lucite, I would think.

And it's just standing on the sand?

No, it's floating. About the height of a person or two persons. Hovering. And you can see through it. There are sand dunes behind and all that.

THE LADDER

It's an ordinary ladder. I can't tell you whether it's aluminum or wood. It's not as shiny as aluminum, but it doesn't look quite like wood, either, so I don't get it. But it's a ladder.

Where?

Oh, it's going from the desert to the cube! Just to the bottom of the cube. A little of it sticks up beyond the bottom, because ladders work that way. You can't step on the top rung and then go to the cube. So the top rung is just above the bottom of the cube.

Leaning against it a little bit?

That's right.

THE HORSE

Arabian! At first it was brown, but the moment I think about it, it would be a black horse. Very black. It's just running around. Near the cube, but not . . . It's in the same picture. In the same image. So it's somewhere around on the desert, running around and underneath the cube, but it doesn't get underneath the cube very much.

THE STORM

Okay, that's way off in the distance. It's a sandstorm. Way off—but you know how things go: You begin to prepare. The horse is prancing around, and I'm calling to the horse and trying to get him in so that I can rein him in and get him to cover.

THE FLOWERS

They're very tiny. The only flowers that I've seen in the desert are down in Death Valley, and these would be tiny flowers in sort of depressions, and they wouldn't be in the same picture that I just saw, the same image I had. I would know they're there because I've been exploring and seen them. But they're not big like sunflowers. They're rather tiny flowers but they're very lovely.

COMMENTS

The cube is you.

Oh, so I'm square? I would've been more comfortable with an ellipse, or something other than . . .

A Native American activist, whose central symbol is the circle of nature, saw the cube as an invading alien form, not as himself at all.

I sympathize with him. I would say that he's right. A hyper-cube, and so forth—there's a lot of that going on right now in physics, and so I didn't object quite that strongly to it, but I would say that it is not me in that sense. It is too square.

It's clear, though. And floating, which suggests living in ideas and intellect.

Ye-esss!

The ladder is your friends.

Really! That's very good. They ground me. But I would say more than friends, that's the lover I'm living with. A lover is more what I use to ground myself.

You anticipated, because the horse is your lover.

Ohhh. Right, and of course the horse is on the ground! If the friends—if the ladder gets me to the horse, that's true historically, because I did get to meet Katherine through my students. The question now is how much that is still a function, whether that ladder is necessary and how much it's necessary. And I think it is, because I think Katherine, the horse would have a lot of trouble just existing by itself. There's some way the horse and the ladder ought to interact to get to the cube. They're both grounded and connect the cube with the ground. Very nice.

Why a black horse?

Oh, because I've had the most wonderful black horse in my life. When I was in high school I had a horse that I trained, and Blackie was its name, a marvelous horse, and it was part Arabian. I love Arabians, and I've ridden Arabians a lot, mostly brown ones, though. So I said originally it was brown, and then I went back to Blackie.

Is that a suitable color for Katherine too?

Well, she's certainly not the ordinary brown. She wears black beautifully. But she also likes bright colors. So we'd have to put a bright blanket on her. *[laughs]* And a lot of ornaments. No, I think black is more striking. And she's certainly striking in her appearance.

Black is mysterious, too, like her writing.

It certainly is.

The storm is trouble, and it's far away; the flowers are children.

Really! Also very tiny, at this point, because there are five children and five grandchildren. But they're at a distance, hopefully, or in valleys, so that I don't have to tend them. Right.

Are you going to use names in your book? I wonder if that's wise. I think what you're getting is wonderful, and I don't see any reason why you shouldn't publish it, except that I'm trying very hard to get my work, which is essentially trying to change paradigms, published, and if something like this gets my name associated with it, then I have even more trouble.

> *Another scientist who's pushing the borders of conventional thinking regretfully declined to be in the book for just that reason!*

Scientists are uptight. I'm trying to change the whole paradigm; in physics it's all *things*. They're just beginning to think in terms of fields. Their equations are field equations, but they still think in terms of quanta and so on. . . . Why don't you just say what the reservations and the problems are, and the penalties that the establishment imposes? Say, look. This is fun, and it may mean something. Why, when we do things like this, should the establishment say, Ahh! The guy's done this, *therefore* he's not a scientist?

Judy Collins

singer/songwriter, Wildflowers, Colors of the Day, Fires of Eden; *author*,
Trust Your Heart *and* Shameless

THE CUBE

In the cube there is a mountain skyline; there is a piano;
there is a blank page, with a beautiful Mont Blanc pen beside it, upon which I can write poetry; and there is a very
simple meal: a flowered plate, like a Limoges plate, on it
there is a bagel, there's a pot of honey, and there's a bar of
soy margarine. *[laughs]* The cube is in the very center of
the landscape, so that you look up and see the horizon, and
you look around you and see the sand, but in front of you is
this cube with these things in it.

The cube is completely transparent?

Yes.

How big?

Oh, it's the size of oneself.

THE LADDER

It's leaning up against the cube, and it's a single ladder, it
goes straight up, and it is made of wood, and it's probably,
mmm, twelve to fifteen feet high.

Yes.

And is the wood old or new?

Oh, it's worn. It's antique, it's had a history. Very old.

THE HORSE
It's a white horse, completely pure white, and it's standing, with its head lifted, and there's a wind blowing, and so its mane is blowing and its tail is blowing, and it's on the other side of the ladder and the cube.

Facing the cube?

It's facing parallel, so that the wind is blowing across the ladder and the cube and also blowing the horse's mane as it faces this wind.

THE STORM
Yes. There is a storm which is a tornado storm, so that it's a whirl? Going up, spiraling, starting tiny on the ground and going way up into the sky, but it stays put and it's in the upper left corner. It creates . . . it must be pulling sand up, because it's colorful, and it gets big from the small, it gets bigger and bigger and bigger. There is a storm center at the top of the left-hand corner, but it doesn't affect anything

that's going on. It creates a little wind that is blowing the horse's mane. But it doesn't disturb the cube or the ladder or the horse. The horse is able to stay put.

It sounds like it's almost rather beautiful.

It *is* beautiful.

THE FLOWERS
There's a cluster of white flowers, but there're also some purple, and the combination is a purple orchid on a stalk and a white gardenia. Very scented. There's a cluster of them, and they're growing out of the right-hand side of the cube.

COMMENTS
The cube is you.

Oh, my!

You put everything you love inside it. It's so cozy in there.

It's *very* cozy.

The ladder is your friends.

Mmm! Good old friends. Well worn. *[laughs]* With a history!

They fit perfectly. Everything you said about what they mean is a perfect fit. The lover being the white horse . . . the white horse is the spiritual horse, you know. The four horses of the Apocalypse, the white is the spiritual search, and of course that's very appropriate because I feel that my life partner is my spiritual partner too. So it is perfect. And the storm, yes, because you see, I'm a great believer in the fact that we all have trouble and that we must keep ourselves distant from it. We must know it's there, and we must understand that it's ours, but we don't have to get in an uproar.

You have children?

I had a child. I have a grandchild. There are many children in my life. Nieces and nephews and . . . lots of them.

Flowers can be something else you nurture, too; they can be creative work.

Yes, of course. The creativity makes great sense. That's beautiful. Beautiful. What a great . . . whatever one calls it. I love it.

Adam Fortunate Eagle

Indian activist, healer, and educator; planner of the Alcatraz Occupation; author, Alcatraz, Alcatraz; *screenwriter,* Scalping Columbus

THE DESERT

I'm looking at it. Right out of my front window. I don't have to imagine.

> *It's very simple: the horizon line, the sand, and the sky.*

I see the mountain range. Off in the distance I can see snow-covered peaks seventy miles away.

THE CUBE

Okay, it's sort of a monolith, somethin' like 2001. We've planted the image of this huge monolith rising out of the desert, shiny black and somehow invested with a certain power, because it dominates the landscape that it's in. It is totally out of character. The landscape, the desert, is soft and flowing and natural. It represents the creative energies of the spirits, whereas the cube represents the dominance of man, with the sharp corners and shininess, which man can do. And he can be totally out of character with his environment instead of being in balance and harmony with it. He's intrusive. And that big, black, shiny cube is intrusive to the landscape. But its presence is certainly noticed. Because it can dominate. And so it has a power in itself.

THE LADDER

Ladders are perceived in different ways by different cultures. In modern society ladders are looked at as a functional utilitarian item, with which to do work around the home and on construction jobs and so forth. But in the mind of ancient peoples, ladders represent a spiritual achievement. By climbing that ladder upwards, you approach the realm of the gods. It then takes on a different character than if it would be around a residence or a shop. A ladder out in the desert would take on a more spiritual significance.

What would it look like?

It'd be made of wood. The kind with rungs on it. The ancient ones had different forms of ladders, not only the two poles with rungs, but massive logs cut with notches that allowed you to climb right up the log. And then the carved log steps evolved into stairways as we know them today.

Where would it be in relation to the cube?

Well, it's goin' from the inside out, from the outside in. Some leaning to the outside so people from the outside could get up and into the cube, and also the reverse: ladders on the inside, leaning against the outer perimeter of the cube, which would have an opening, something similar to a kiva, so the people can emerge from the interior to the exterior. And that can also symbolize the balance of that energy that is created by the cube.

THE HORSE

Easy, easy. Out here, of course, I would relate to my own horse, an Appaloosa called Man. As opposed to the movie where they had a man called Horse. Because we want people to perceive things differently when they move out here. And so I can see my horse, Man. I sold him a few years back 'cause my feeding pasture is no longer available. They put a house on it, so Man suffers from the encroachment of society. I haven't seen him in years, but he's out there somewhere, I'm sure.

Where is he in this picture?

Well, I don't think he'd relate to that cube very much at all. Naahh. Man would be totally indifferent—the horse called

Man. Because the cube doesn't represent anything in a horse's mind, horse sense, as we call it, that would have any bearing on his existence, or being. It's totally unrelated to Man.

THE STORM

That's easy out here. We can see the storms coming at a distance, as the winds that precede the storm start churning up the landscape, and those winds pick up dust and sand. All we do is look out in the desert, and we can watch the storm approach. We just saw one last week here.

Where is the storm in the picture?

Well, I would like to think that storms are somewhat distant. It's better to look at a storm at a distance than to be in the middle of one. It's nice to look at, but it's not nice to be in it.

THE FLOWERS

Could be occurring in the springtime, when the severe nightly freezing, the hard frost, is ended. Today, we have in the middle of February weather in the 60s, which is way, way above average. And that sends out a false signal to all the little plants and insects, who think, "Boy! Spring has arrived!" And little flowers start budding out, lulled by this false spring. But the reality of the seasons will set in very shortly. By next week, suddenly winter returns with full vengeance, and all these little fellows that were lulled into a false sense of security will find that their world ends for them very dramatically and suddenly. And the other guys, the procrastinators, will say, "See? I told you so." *[laughs]* "You little early birds, you went out there and bit the dust. You should've laid back and just waited," waited for the natural order of things, the real thing with the moon cycles and the sunrise moving north, when spring really does arrive, and all these little guys can make the emergence into the world and not fear being frozen to death.

If you put flowers in this picture, would they be the premature ones or the prudent ones?

I would prefer them to be the ones who waited for the natural order of life. Then they have a chance of survival. If you take it out of the order of life, they run the risk of rather severe death. Like the cube itself, out of order, out of balance with its environment, may suffer from that windstorm that is approaching. Because it has flat walls and sides, it will take on the brunt of that wind a lot easier than the soft curves of a sand dune. The sand dunes will give and yield and blow with the wind. The cube will not. And if the wind is strong enough, it'll blow the cube over.

They're all over the place. They don't relate to that cube any more than the horse did.

COMMENTS

Looks like you're going to turn this game inside out.
Because that cube doesn't seem like you at all.

No. That's right. It's man's imposition on our environment, rather than blending and fitting and adapting and being in balance with it. It is intrusive as man is intrusive.

So these symbols aren't universal! The Cube comes
from Europe, and before that, from the Middle East.
The Ka'ab where they worship in Mecca is a cube.

And ours is the circle. See? I have the Roundhouse Gallery, I have the Earth Lodge Museum. They're all circles! Not cubes. Nature does not make cubes. Man has to make the cube.

Our belief system was that the earth was the mother and the provider of all life forms that the Great Spirit created. And we are not superior to anything out there, we are a part of the total. Even though we have spirituality, it was not in the sense of organized religion. That came from the east. Religions are an invention of man, a belief system that becomes intrusive on others. "If you don't believe as I believe, I have the right to kill you." Catholicism and Islam have done all that—murdered millions of people on the earth mother just because they don't believe as I believe. So it's again like the cube, an intrusive and a *dominant* force. Just like that cube wanted to dominate the scene in the desert, those religious beliefs want to dominate the earth and all the people on it. But religion throughout the history of man has changed constantly. We've had all kinds of gods on the earth, long before Christianity and Islam came along. In terms of the global time frame, all these are recent phenomena. When you look at the lifetime of man on this planet, three million years, the last two thousand years is no more than the steam of a buffalo's breath in wintertime.

Our way is to live in balance and harmony with every living thing, because all living things are our relations. Not to dominate, control, and all of that. The cube dominates and controls.

Is there anything of you in that cube?

No!

If you were a form, what would it be?

See, I would be like the animals, the birds, and the flowers around it. I would be indifferent to the cube.

But the ladder opens up the cube, somehow.

It opens up the cube, and it's like opening up Pandora's box, because you don't know what the hell the cube is gonna do to you or you are going to do within the cube. If you go into the cube, you go into conformity. Because the four walls and the floor and ceiling that surround you are squares and corners, and you are trapped, forced to conform to those limitations and parameters. And the only escape is that ladder. And so you go up and out of that cube and down the sides of the cube on another ladder. It either lets you in or it lets you out, depends on where a person is coming from. Do you want to be stuck in a cube and conform to all the belief systems society is going to impose on you?

There's something of you in that ladder. You're help-ing people get out of the cube.

That's what happens in the sweat lodge. We held a sweat lodge yesterday for a group of Vietnam veterans who've gone through horrible experiences and still have that post-traumatic syndrome. The sweat lodge provided a ladder, be-cause these wounded veterans were trapped in the cube. The cube in this instance was their own mind and memo-ries. They had agonized with these memories of tragedy and horror for twenty-five years. And they had this survivor's guilt complex. And that guilt complex is the cube. It boxes you in and you can't escape. You're not free because your guilt keeps you there. And so the ladder, then, is put down into that hole in the top of the cube. And it allows these people to come out and to see, to see the universe, to see the totality of life around it, and how life is a one-time miracle. Through the medium of your grandparents, and then your parents, here you are, and you're going to be here just for a limited period of time. But now *you* become a parent, and you are creating a miracle itself when your children come along. And so, by the most remarkable of coincidences, each of us has taken our place in this ladder of time.

The horse is your lover.

That's why these women today look at a hunk of a guy and say, "Man, isn't he a stud?" They wish! In their dreams! But not mine. Nope, I look at him not in that way at all. Man was my friend. And he was his own individual personality. He could be as nice as he wanted to be, and other times he could be just as cantankerous and stubborn. Sometimes I had to assert my will and say, "Hey, I've got a job to do, and you're going to help me." Then I would have to assert my authority over my friend, but because we had a purpose, not just because I wanted to show my domination over the horse. Only when it was necessary.

Not a bad model for human relations, like with a mate.

Yeah. *[laughs]* That's right, because you've got to let that person be their individual self. Not dominate and control all the time. *[His wife calls him.]*

We're having more company coming in. Now two of my young warriors, my grandsons, are just coming in also. The young warriors are being taught the traditional ways. Two weeks ago when we went to do a show in California, the young warriors did their own sweat lodge. And none of them was over fifteen. So they're growing up appreciating and understanding these things and learning.

The flowers are children.

Hold on, I'm gonna holler at them. . . . You just heard me give the young warriors an assignment, to take care of the company, and that is shared responsibility. And when we do ceremony, I always get the young people involved as much as I can. So that not only is it shared responsibility, but for the young ones it becomes a learning opportunity by doing, rather than just watching from the sidelines. There shouldn't be any spectators to life. We're all involved in it.

The Vocubulary

Imagining your cube (and ladder, horse, storm, and flowers) was surprisingly easy, but *interpreting* it may have given you some trouble. Decoding the imagination's mysterious images is a skill that takes practice. The Sufis call it *tasvir:* the art of interpreting pictures.

Well, what does it *mean?* people sometimes want to know after playing The Cube. The right answer to that question is, *You* tell *me.* But that's not a very satisfying answer. Dream dictionaries (those little books that say if you dream of a fish, you're going to get married) are usually wrong; they are also immensely beloved. Most of us could use a little help with our personal *tasvir.*

While we cannot tell you for sure what your cube means, we can tell you what many types of cubes (ladders, horses, and so forth) have meant to hundreds of others who have played the game. The result is The Vocubulary: a compromise between the absolute uniqueness of each cube and the cozy inspiration of dream dictionaries.

HOW TO USE THE VOCUBULARY

Listed here—in alphabetical order—are many possible qualities of cubes, ladders, horses, storms, and flowers. Look up the key traits of your cube (or other element): its size, material, color, position, distance. (If your cube is so unique that you can't find it here, choose the closest approximations.) For each trait, you'll find a cluster of possible meanings, drawn from the hundreds of times we have played The Cube and from our own intuition. Don't take these as the end, but as the beginning of understanding your cube.

Do any of the listed meanings ring true for you? (Note that they may be contradictory: a cube standing on its edge, for instance, could be "balanced" or "wobbly." The same image may mean opposite things to different people—or even to the same person.) Or are some of them at least "getting warm," leading you in the right direction?

If not, trust your feeling. Don't try to force your cube into the mold of an ill-fitting interpretation. The Vocubulary can cover only a small fraction of possible cubes; it can never be complete, because individuality is infinite. Think of it as a work in endless progress to which you contribute. Try some of the following techniques for feeling out the unique truth of *your* cube. Then add it to The Vocubulary. (We'd like to hear about it.)

- Ask your friends, lover, and family what *they* see in your cube's imagery. People who know you well can often give you missing pieces of the puzzle.
- Free-associate. *Anything* that pops into your head in connection with your cube (horse, ladder, etc.), however random it seems, is a vital clue to what that image means to you. Follow the trail!
- Play with adjectives. If your cube is metal, for instance, you might say, "This metal is hard, it's bright, it's reflective, it's refined, it's stressed . . . " You're describing yourself.
- Consider jokes and puns. The imagination has a sense of humor. While flying horses often represent magic or purity, one man who saw a flying horse was in love with a flight attendant! A woman wondered why her ladder was steel when everyone else in her family had friendly old wooden ladders. Then she remembered that her best friend's last name is Steele.
- Consult body-sense. Feel your cube's position and material from within, kinesthetically. What images come to mind? A cube on edge might "feel like" a daredevil kid—or poised cat—walking the top of a fence; a cube on its point might remind you of a ballet dancer; an edge-first cube could suggest

the wave-cutting prow of a ship. What do these images mean to you? You can also "feel" the physical qualities and closeness or distance of your ladder, horse, storm, and flowers.

- Respect mystery. Remember that any image is far more than the sum of its interpretations. No matter how many insights you take out of your cube, it remains intact, a mysterious companion and wordless reflection of your life.

The cube

IF YOUR CUBE IS . . . YOU ARE . . .

ABOVE THE HORIZON

idealistic
intellectual
spiritual
a dreamer

AIR

open
undefended
self-effacing
subtle

BELOW THE HORIZON

practical
worldly
down-to-earth
sensual

BISECTING THE HORIZON

visionary and
    practical
spiritual and sensual
making ideas/ideals
    practical

BLACK

stylish
stark
mysterious
guarded
self-contained
drawn to the dark
    side

BLUE

serene
cool
spiritual
electric
loyal
distant
aloof
sad

BROWN

earthy
warm
serious
studious

BURIED, PARTIALLY

keeping a low profile
lying in ambush
camouflaged
deep-rooted
overwhelmed

CLOSE

comfortable with
    closeness
a "people person"
family-focused
impulsive
living in the present
concerned with the
    actual

CLOUD

in a world of your
    own
a dreamer
imaginative
pure

CRYSTAL

visionary
spiritual
pure
clear

DIAMOND

brilliant
precious
rare
lucid
sparkling
cutting
of firm, decisive
    opinions
indestructible
multifaceted

DICE

a gambler in life
a risk-taker
lucky

DIFFERENT ON EACH SIDE

many-sided
complex
versatile
changeable
self-aware

DISTANT

protective of your
    "space"
independent
taking the long view
seeing things in
    perspective
abstract

DUG INTO THE SAND

rooted
stubborn
conservative
opinionated

EDGE FACING FRONT

aggressive
assertive
energetic
an "action" person
dual-natured (two
    faces show)

EDGE, STANDING ON

an immigrant
a traveler, transient
between two worlds
undecided
edgy
discriminating
precise
balanced
precarious
daredevil
cutting-edge

FABRIC

pliable
domestic
homespun
textured
cultured
integrating many
    influences

FAR AWAY

(see distant)

FLOATING

optimistic
idealistic
spiritual
living in ideas or
    fantasy
impractical
"above it all"

FOOD (CHEESE, JELL-O, BREAD, ETC.)

nurturing
giving
devoured by others
sensual, pleasure-
    loving

FORMICA

tidy
cheerful
able to start afresh
upwardly mobile

GLASS, CLEAR

clear-minded
candid
self-revealing
realistic
fragile

GLASS, COLORED

imaginative
romantic
poetic
seeing what you want
    to see

GLASS, GREENHOUSE/TERRARIUM

cultivating inner life
displaying inner life
protective
possessive

GLASS, SHATTERPROOF

tougher than you
    look

GLASS, STAINED

(see colored)
spiritual
religious
a craftsperson
nostalgic
artistic

GOLD

valuable
weighty
refined
loyal, true
desirable
rich

GRAY

conservative
neutral
fair, just
ambivalent
factual
subtle
bored

GREEN

hopeful
optimistic
ever-reviving
nature-loving
ecologically aware
grass-smoker
wealthy

HAND-SIZED

intimate
affectionate
trusting
practical

HOLE IN THE GROUND

deep
introverted
attuned to the
    unconscious
nonconformist
depressed

HOLLOW

spacious
receptive
light-hearted
objective
protective

HOLOGRAM

elusive
disembodied
speculative
futuristic

HOUSE

nurturing
practical
domestic
socially conscious
in real estate

HOVERING

tentative
uncommitted
realistic, but open to
    possibility

HUGE

confident
egoistic
dominant
grandiose
generous

ICE, MELTING

vulnerable
calm
refreshing
in love

ICE, MELT-PROOF

imperturbably cool
resourceful
intrepid
rational

JACK-IN-THE-BOX

humorous
full of surprises
more than meets the
    eye

JELL-O

(see food)
vulnerable
timid
tender
nurturing
funny

LARGE

confident
capable
capacious
healthily egoistic

METAL FRAMEWORK (WITH GLASS, CLOTH, ETC.)

having basic strength
    of character

METAL, HOLLOW

self-protective
tough-skinned
cynical
venturesome

METAL, SOLID

made strong by stress
weighty
introverted
impenetrable
melancholy

MIDDLE DISTANCE

(see close and distant)
balanced between
    extremes

MIRRORED

reflecting others
a realist
visually oriented

MULTICOLORED

multitalented
multi-ethnic
versatile
moody

NEAR

(see close)

OASIS

hospitable
nurturing
welcoming
pleasure-loving

ON THE SAND

down-to-earth
practical
commonsensical
reality-oriented
concerned with the
    tangible

OPAQUE

private
self-protective
enigmatic

ORIGINAL MATERIAL (AN AMBERLIKE RESIN, A SPACESHIP METAL, A RIGID FABRIC, ETC.)

unusual
solitary
different
self-made
self-aware

OUTLINED (LINES ON EDGES)

clearly defined
firm about your
    boundaries

PAPER

vulnerable
trying out an identity
playful
bluffing (if large)

PLASTIC

of blue-collar origin
unpretentious
proud to be ordinary
"salt of the earth"

PLEXIGLAS

(see glass and plastic)
resilient
invisibly shielded

POINT, STANDING ON

special, exceptional
unconventional
fastidious
spiritual
poised
balanced
centered
ready to take flight
diamondlike

PURPLE

regal
luxury-loving
extravagant
pensive
moderate
immoderate
romantic
wise

PYRAMID

interested in power
(worldly or
spiritual)
mysterious
more than meets the
eye (a cube half-
buried)

RAINBOW

multitalented
tolerant
optimistic
childlike

RED

warm-hearted
hot-tempered
passionate
courageous
aggressive
revolutionary

REFLECTING THE SUN

ambitious
emulating someone
great
religious

ROLLING/TUMBLING

uncommitted
changeable
rootless
nomadic
searching

RUBBER

tough but not hard
resilient
able to bounce back
flexible
funny

RUBIK'S

complex
adaptable
versatile
ingenious
challenging/enjoying
challenge
liking to match wits

SHINY

bright
attention-getting
achievement-oriented
excelling at what you
do

SMALL

modest
keeping a low profile
extroverted
realistic in
expectations

SOLID

substantial
secure
consistent
honest
unintrospective
full of unexpressed
feelings

SPINNING

intense
busy
high-energy
elusive

SPONGE

curious
thirsty for knowledge
easily influenced

STONE, BLOCKS

the sum of many
    experiences
a work in progress
self-made

STONE, ONE PIECE

(see solid)
monumental
unchanging
firm
hard to influence
stubborn
self-declaring ("Here
    I stand")
enduring
resigned

STONE, POLISHED

smooth
refined
ambitious

STONE, ROUGH

natural
honest, blunt
awkward
unpolished

TINY

concentrated
focused
hidden
precious

TRANSLUCENT

thoughtful
meditative
receptive to
    inspiration
selective
enigmatic
alluring

TRANSPARENT

candid
unable to hide
    feelings
self-revealing
observant
objective

TURNING

moody
multifaceted
active

TWO CUBES

a strongly dual
    personality
physically ill

WATER

emotional
mystical
fluid
sensitive
full of potential
close to the
    unconscious

YELLOW, BRIGHT

cheerful
upbeat
making people happy

The ladder

(note: for colors, see under the cube)

IF YOUR LADDER IS . . . YOUR FRIENDS . . .

ACCESS TO CUBE'S ENTRANCE

know the way into
 your heart
are the only ones you
 let in
help you know
 yourself
evoke your emotions

ACCESS TO CUBE'S TOP

help you reach your
 full potential

ALUMINUM

provide practical help
work with you
are unsentimental
 utilitarian
 up-to-date
 reliable
 light yet strong
 never a burden

ASCENDING

(see reaching into the
 sky)

BALSA WOOD

are fair-weather
 friends
can't be relied on
are your own
 thoughts
are angels
 (imaginary/
 spiritual friends)

BRANCHES

are natural
 outdoor types
 rough-hewn
 your relatives
 uprooted
 dead

BREAD

are nourishing
are eating/drinking
 buddies

BROKEN

have betrayed you
let you down
are in trouble
are estranged from
 you

BUILT INTO THE CUBE'S SIDE

are your siblings
are close as family

CACTUS

are difficult and
 prickly

CONNECTING CUBE TO GROUND

bring you down to
 earth
ground you in reality
are your anchor

DESCENDING FROM THE SKY

include God, higher
    power
are from a different
    milieu
are influential
    contacts
are spiritually evolved
can help you rise

DESCENDING INTO THE GROUND

go deeply into life
help your self-
    understanding
like to explore
    mysteries
like the lower depths
are undermining you
are going straight to
    hell

DIFFERENT MATERIAL FROM CUBE

are unlike you

EXTENSION (LIKE A FIRE ENGINE'S)

keep increasing in
    number
have a long reach
are resourceful
come through in
    emergency
save your life

FAR FROM THE CUBE

are not very close
live far from you
don't see you often
are not important to
    you

FEW RUNGS

are just a few

FLOATING

are dreamers
    drifters
    intellectuals
    philosophers
    artists
    valued for their
        ideas
    not very practical

FLOATING ABOVE THE CUBE

hover over you
protect you

FOLDED

(see stepladder)

FOLDING, JOINTED (MANY POSITIONS)

are clever
    versatile
    adaptable
    ingenious

FREESTANDING, DIAGONAL

have a unique slant
    on things
are forward-looking
    (if toward
    horizon)
are nonconformists

FREESTANDING, VERTICAL

are independent
don't lean on you (or
    you on them)
are ambitious
are "upstanding"
have your respect

GOLD

are priceless to you
are loyal

INSIDE CUBE

are in your heart
are in your
    confidence
are intimates
are protected by you
find you possessive

INSIDE & OUTSIDE CUBE

are of two kinds:
    intimates and
    acquaintances

IRON

are "heavyweights"
    strong
    blunt
    loyal
    uneducated
    serious, somber

IRON, WROUGHT

are cultured
    creative
    artistic
have worked on
    themselves

LEANING AGAINST CUBE

lean on you
give you support
are close to you
touch you

LEATHER THONGS

are natural, organic
    athletic
    Western
    casual
    outdoorsy
    plainspoken
    strong but supple

LIBRARY LADDER

like to read
lead you to
    knowledge
are writers, teachers
are well-informed
    cultured
    polished
travel a lot

LYING DOWN

are relaxed
    casual
    companions in
    leisure
    tired
    not much use
    (unless in
    emergency)
    down and out
    deadbeats
    sick
    dead

MANY RUNGS

are many

METAL

(*see aluminum, iron, steel*)

MISSING RUNGS

you've lost close ones

PAINT-SPATTERED

are your creative
    collaborators
have had varied
    experiences

REACHING INTO THE SKY

include God, higher
    power
help you evolve
    spiritually
help you achieve
    ambitions

REACHING TOP OF CUBE

(*see access*)

RICKETY

are unreliable
    in bad shape
    ill or aging

ROOTED IN THE SAND

are rooted
    immovably loyal
take a firm stand
give strong support

ROPE

are flexible
    dependent
have a strong bond
    with you
reach out to you
are travelers

SAME HEIGHT AS CUBE

are your equals

SAME MATERIAL AS CUBE

are very much like
    you

SHORTER THAN CUBE

are not quite your
    equals

SPIRAL

come and go
are on-again, off-
    again
help you
    intermittently

STEEL

are steadfastly reliable
    made strong by
    stress
    indestructible
    straightforward
    streamlined
    practical
    unadorned

STEPLADDER, FOLDED

come through when
    you need them
don't live up to their
    potential

STEPLADDER, OPEN

are stable
    steady
    dependable
    independent
    self-reliant
    in couples
    in two groups

SUPPORTING CUBE (OFF THE GROUND)

support you
    completely
are your foundation
are necessary to your
    life

SWIMMING-POOL LADDER

are playmates
share your fun and
    leisure
help you relax
lead you into your
    feelings

TALLER THAN CUBE

are people you look
    up to

WOOD, FINISHED

are cultured
    educated
care about
    appearances
are aristocratic
    wealthy
    snobbish

WOOD, NEW

are fairly new friends

WOOD, OLD

are old friends
    familiar and
        comfortable
    older than you

The horse

IF YOUR HORSE IS . . . YOUR LOVER IS . . .

APPALOOSA

American
Western
casual

ARABIAN

high-strung
aristocratic
elegant
sensitive
nervous
proud

ASCENDING THE LADDER

rising in your
     estimation
ambitious
spiritually evolving

BEHIND THE CUBE

backing you up
in the background of
     your life
the power behind the
     throne
protected by you
hiding behind you
taking a backseat
"behind" in age or
     career
in the past

BESIDE THE CUBE

your equal
     companion
loyal
close

BLACK

mysterious
romantic
powerful
moody
a good lover
brunet

BRIDLED/SADDLED (ORNATE)

romantic
exotic
adventurous
chivalrous
a crusader
regal
wealthy

BRIDLED/SADDLED (PLAIN LEATHER)

married
responsible
hard-working
domesticated

BROWN

warm
earthy
sensual
ordinary,
     unpretentious
brunet
African-American
Hispanic

CAMEL

enduring
reliable
long-married
bearing burdens
    capably

CIRCLING THE CUBE

revolving around you

CLYDESDALE (THE BUDWEISER HORSE)

a real workhorse
big, heavy
substantial
physically strong

DEAD

deceased
no longer loved

DESCENDING THE LADDER

falling in your esteem
no longer idealized

FAR FROM THE CUBE

in another city/
    country
indifferent
very independent
in his/her own world
a low priority for you
on the way out of
    your life

FEMALE

(see mare)

FLYING HORSE

a new love
idealized
idealistic
admired, looked up
    to
spiritual
intellectual
magical
taking you higher
taking you away

FRIGHTENED BY THE STORM

easily upset
a worrier
having problems
    right now

HEAD DOWN

relaxed
fulfilling his/her
    needs
a browser
braced for trouble
depressed

HOOFPRINTS ONLY

a memory

HUNGRY/THIRSTY

not getting enough
    from you

INSIDE THE CUBE

in your heart of
    hearts
helping you find
    yourself
in your
    protection/shelter
jealously possessed

LICKING THE CUBE

nourished by you
demonstrative
a good kisser
a good lover

LOOKING AT THE STORM

a worrier
vigilant, protective

LOST

unsure of direction in
    life
separated from you

LYING DOWN

relaxed
secure
at home
lazy
ill
refusing to budge

MALE

(see stallion)

MANY HORSES

(see two or more)

MARE

nurturing
gentle
patient
fertile
enduring
temperamental

MUSTANG

wild
tough
a "street kid"
self-reliant
rebellious
a troublemaker

NAKED (NO SADDLE OR BRIDLE)

free
loved sexually

NEAR THE CUBE

close to you
loyal
committed

NEAR THE LADDER

your best friend
a friend before a lover
close to your friends

NERVOUS

sensitive
high-strung
temperamental
easily upset

NO HORSE

nonexistent
gone
shut out of your
    solitary soul

ON TOP OF CUBE

dominant
honored
on a pedestal
possessed by you

PALOMINO

your pal
fair (in any sense)
good as gold
blond

PEGASUS

(see flying horse)

PINTO

friendly
versatile
moody
artistic
the object of mixed
    feelings

PONY

small
cute
childlike
affectionate

PRANCING

proud
spirited
eager
energetic
theatrical
affected

RIDDEN BY SOMEONE

rational, controlled
goal-oriented
hard-working
involved with
    someone else

RIDDEN BY YOU

your spouse
relied on by you
your close
    companion
taking you where you
    want to go

RUNNING

busy
active
energetic
preoccupied
athletic

RUNNING AWAY

leaving you
undependable
uncommitted

SADDLED

(see bridled)

SPOTTED

(see pinto)

STALLION

bold
assertive
adventurous
dominant
protective
proud

STANDING

calm
patient
content with
    him/herself
principled
committed
not doing much

STANDING OVER
(SMALL) CUBE

dominant
framing your life

THIRSTY

(see hungry)

THOROUGHBRED

well-bred
competitive
a high achiever
very good-looking

TIED UP

married ("hitched")
committed
not free

TOY HORSE

a plaything
a possession
toyed with
not taken seriously

TROJAN HORSE

pregnant
having an affair
bent on conquest
treacherous
bringing unpleasant
    in-laws

TROTTING

determined
goal-directed
mannerly
well-coordinated

TWO OR MORE HORSES

more than one lover
dual-natured
multifaceted
moody

UNDER THE CUBE (LARGE OR ON ITS POINT)

dominated by you
in your shadow
under your
    protection
clinging

UNICORN

enchanting
unworldly
shy
pure
innocent
spiritual
magical

WALKING

calm
casual
taking his/her time
determined

WHITE

idealized
idealistic
your dream
of high principles
good

WINGED

(see flying horse)

The storm

IF YOUR STORM IS . . . TROUBLE IS . . .

ABOVE THE CUBE

here, now
in your childhood
kept to yourself
affecting only you

ACID RAIN

nagging worries

APPROACHING

not here yet
in the foreseeable
    future

BEAUTIFUL

challenging
inspiring
part of life's drama

BEHIND THE CUBE

in your past
ignored by you

BLACK CLOUDS

worries
threatening but not
    actual

BLOWING AWAY THE CUBE

devastating
a major
    disappointment
failure
loss
illness
a strong sense of
    mortality

BLOWING AWAY THE LADDER

much worse for your
    friends

BURYING THE CUBE

overwhelming
transforming
humbling
a learning experience

BURYING THE HORSE

overwhelming your
    lover

COMING

(see approaching)

DEPARTING

over for now

ELECTRICAL

shocking
galvanizing
giving you a jolt
illuminating
enlightening

FAR AWAY

minimal
nothing to worry
    about

FRIGHTENING THE HORSE

upsetting your lover

HORIZON, ON THE

in the distant future
other people's
on the evening news

LOCALIZED

confined to part of
    life
manageable
intermittent

LIGHTNING

(see electrical)

OUT OF SIGHT

absent from your life
    now
vigorously denied

PAST

in your past
the worst is over

RAINSTORM

an emotional crisis
bringing tears
dampening your
    spirits
depressing
breaking the tension
necessary for growth

SANDSTORM

blinding, confusing
irritating
life-changing
a financial or
    material crisis

THUNDER

quarrels
just sound and fury
threatening
rumored

TORNADO	WIND	
violent	a spiritual crisis	bringing change
destructive	stressful	energizing
focused, acute	upsetting routines	renewing
	chaotic	

The flowers

IF YOUR FLOWERS ARE . . . CHILDREN ARE . . .

AROUND THE HORSE'S NECK

your lover's pride/
    prize/
    triumph

BEHIND THE CUBE

protected by you
your followers/
    students
grown and left home

BEHIND THE HORSE

coming, once you
    find love
protected by your
    lover

BOUQUET

close to one another
close together in age
gifts to/from your
    lover

BRIGHT-COLORED

bright
important to you
attention-getting
sources of pleasure

CACTUS FLOWERS

a lot of trouble
worth the trouble
hardy

CLOSE TO THE CUBE

your own
young
under your
    protection

CUT FLOWERS

adopted
stepchildren
grown, left home

DAISIES

innocent
natural
fresh
blond

DEAD FLOWERS

in trouble
estranged from you
of no interest to you
deceased or aborted
grown up, on their
    own

FALLING FROM THE SKY/STORM

blessings
worth the trouble
works of art

FAR FROM THE CUBE

other people's
not a part of your life
living far away

FLOATING IN THE AIR

unconceived
undecided on
future children

FOREGROUND, IN THE

very important to you

GARDEN, AWAY FROM CUBE

someone else's

GARDEN, NEAR CUBE

your own
kept safe
cherished, cultivated

INSIDE THE CUBE

wished for
in the womb
young
dependent
cherished
overprotected
possessed
an extension of
    yourself

MANY FLOWERS

many kids
your life's work
other people's

OASIS, IN AN

protected from harsh
    life
given enriched
    environment
sources of hope

ON OR NEAR THE LADDER

your best friends
your friends' kids
nieces, nephews

ROSES

passionately loved
children of passionate
    love

SMALL

young
underfoot
pets
other people's
not a big part of your
    life

TREE, ON OR UNDER

growing on their own
entrusted to life

UNDER THE HORSE

protected by your
    lover

VASE, IN

your pride
cherished
on display
possessed

WATER LILIES

close to the
    unconscious
close to their mother
pure

WILD, GROWING

not your
    responsibility
entrusted to life

The Origin of The Cube

In Three Chapters

CHAPTER 1

In the summer of 1987, on the remote island of Korcula in the Adriatic archipelago, scattered all over a small private beach, sunbathing naked and our senses dulled under the hot Mediterranean sun, my longtime friends "Cubed" me for the first time. They asked the questions, and I lazily answered without paying too much attention to their giggling or occasional hearty laughter. When they told me the answers, I thought The Cube was just another game we played that year. Anyway, nobody knew where it came from. The smell of summer laziness was everywhere, and not much further thought was given to The Cube, with the occasional exception of its use as a part of another game, the constant exercise of Mediterranean seduction.

Nevertheless, many cubes were collected during that happy summer of 1987.

CHAPTER 2

A couple of months later, in late September, gathering energy for the final cut of my first film, I spent some time at my grandmother's house in Vojvodina, the northern part of Yugoslavia. I've always thought that the small village on the bank of the Danube was an unusual oasis of calm, bypassed by politics and wars, and that the locals were mere observers of history, although their habits were deeply rooted in Austro-Hungarian tradition. Every aspect of local life revealed the strong influence of that long-forgotten but once mighty empire. Especially the way people offered and served food. My grandmother was no exception.

One afternoon, after the customary rich and endless lunch, being constantly bugged by her questions why I am not—and when do I think I will get—married, I tried to change the subject by playing The Cube with her. To my astonishment she said,

"Never mind my cube. You tell me your horse so I can fix you up with a nice girl in the village."

My eyes opened wide.

"What? You know this game?"

She answered with the air of something obvious.

"Of course I know. Everybody knows it. And it's not a game! Just tell me your horse and I'll tell you . . . "

"Wait! Where does it come from? Where did you learn it?"

"Oh, it's a long story, and I've got to feed the chickens."

She left me alone and intrigued. The only person who could tell me more without asking for my marriage plans was the local priest. So I paid him a visit. No, not at the church. I found him at his usual fishing spot where the Danube slows down, making a sharp turn. A bottle of local red was enough to release me from most of my sins.

I knew Father Ambrosie, and he knew me. He said I was the only one who had showed no respect for his baptizing technique, splashing water all over the church and crying my lungs out. I bet he told that to everyone. Anyway, he was in a good mood despite the fact that he hadn't caught any fish. He smiled at me . . . or the bottle of local red.

"What's the bribe for?" He took a long swig. "The Cube? The Turks brought it! Anyway, that's my theory. Other people have other theories, but I disagree. If you go through the church books way back to the beginning of the last century, you find nothing but the usual records of births and deaths, [swig] just like any small town or village on the outskirts of the Empire . . . [swig] except for a brief period of about twenty years, when the usual records of life in the village . . . you know how they wrote those things, in a stuffy gilded style so it could be preserved for generations and . . . Where was I? [swig] Ah, yes, that carefully maintained tradition suddenly turned into a random account of events in the form of a diary." He looked at me conspiratorially and paused.

I wasn't a film director anymore; I was a kid waiting for a story.

[Swig] "In the beginning, the diary has clear statements about a series of events that took place in our village. First in the usual German, then in Serbian, then later in Arabic, Sanskrit, and finally in some incomprehensible language which still puzzles scholars in Heidelberg and Oxford. [pause and swig] The diary," he continued, "starts with the description of an unusual humidity in the summer of 1804 which, according to the writing, was so thick that the whole village vanished in the fog for several days. Some horses, children, and old men got lost, never to be found." He crossed himself and took another swig. "When it cleared he was already there. Made out of fog."

"Who?"

"Kariton, the man who brought The Cube!"

"He was a Turk? Doesn't sound Turkish."

"Well, some people thought he was. I think he was a Greek who stole The Cube from the Turks and fled across the border. His name was actually Hariton, but nobody could pronounce that *H* correctly, so they named him Kariton. Besides, it sounded more Christian to them. [swig] Anyway, if you read further, Hariton or Kariton, whatever you call him, organized the village according to The Cube. And the village prospered.

It became the center of the world." He gazed into the sunset nostalgically.

I tried to imagine the tiny village as the center of anything, but it was hard. He turned toward me.

"You don't believe me? Read the diary. Everything's there. [swig] The village didn't immediately become the center, of course. First it was a stopping point for caravans which, for some reason, changed their thousand-year routes. All the languages of the world were spoken. Then schools and bordellos were built. Temples, mosques, synagogues, and churches of all kinds popped up everywhere, and when they didn't serve their gods, they served the others—the gods of trade. Mountains of finest Chinese silk were traded for huge Russian diamonds, tons of Spanish gold, or tall Arabic ships full of coffee and Oriental spices. Everything and everybody made a stopover at the village, which wasn't a village anymore."

"It wasn't? What happened?"

"It swelled into a beautiful European metropolis."

I thought, smiling, what a wonderful liar. He wants to place this small village somewhere in history.

"What happened to K . . . Hariton?"

"Oh, he found his horse, I mean wife, and got married. I've forgotten her name, but they had four children. Two boys and two girls. When he died the family left, taking The Cube with them. And the center of the world followed and moved elsewhere. We became a tiny village again."

"But people in the village, I mean the city, knew the answers. Why . . . ?"

"They knew the answers, yes! The proper interpretation, no! Even after all these years we are still learning. [swig]"

"What's there to learn?"

"Oh-ho-ho, what! Many, many things you don't even know exist in you and your friends. [swig] For example, do you know that some major political and historical events of our times, and I'm not talking centuries, I'm talking thousands of years, were rightly or wrongly made in consultation with The Cube? Major wars were won and lost—Caesar, Napoleon, Kutuzov, even the Russian revolution. [swig] Even an art movement was named after The Cube!"

I started laughing. He was smiling himself, enjoying his story or maybe the wine.

"What? You don't believe me?"

"No, no, I believe you, but how come of all these center-of-the-world activities, nothing's left in the village?"

A long swig emptied the bottle.

"You know what? You're scaring my fish with all these Cube questions. Come back tomorrow, bring some more wine, and I'll show you the diary."

Well, tomorrow was another day, and destiny wanted me back at my editing table so I could finish my film, but I promised I'd be back to learn more about the diary. Father Ambrosie just waved the empty bottle for a goodbye. That was the last time I saw him.

CHAPTER 3

A few years and many more cubes later I'm in the city of New York, waiting for Hollywood to return my phone calls.

"Knock, knock." Destiny knocks on my door in the form of Annie, Big Jacques, and fourteen cats.

Annie: (grinning) Hi! We're your neighbors.

Jacques: (commanding) Annie! Stop talking and feed him first! We can't allow any skinny neighbors here!

The cats don't comment, but one of them, Mr. Coby (the biggest, fattest Russian Blue I've ever seen), looks at me, blinks twice, turns to Jacques, and, I swear, mumbles something like, "The skinny guy's okay!"

They storm the apartment.

As for me, I was speechless, which was understood as hungry. Maybe I was. In no time I found myself in the middle of a gourmet feast that could have been modestly described as a Roman food orgy of wild proportions, surrounded by fourteen cats, Annie asking me questions, and Jacques answering them instead. I was still speechless, most of the time. The food was so good that it took me a while to figure out who they are.

Annie is better than Prozac and Valium combined. You talk to her once or twice daily, and your depression is gone. A sudden burst of energy fills you up, and you can again breathe normally, even here in New York City. Your brain becomes more agile, like after taking some verbal ginseng. I strongly recommend daily doses of Annie's talking. You'll feel better, guaranteed!

Big (and that's a modest description) Jacques is her husband. I personally think they are both lying about that, and that B I G Jacques is actually her genie who buried the magic lamp as soon as he got out of it. He's the cook!

The cats are the cats, with the exception of Mr. Coby, who smokes cigars in my bathroom and bursts into occasional laughter for no apparent reason.

Of course, I played The Cube with all of them (including the cats), and they played with their friends, and their friends played with their friends, and so on until, after many dinners, one very good screenplay, and so many cubes collected, I thought we should publish *The Cube* and tell *you* what we know.

I have to tell you that Annie actually wrote the book and that I, apart from sharing some of the cubes from my collection, was mostly the provider of the second-hand smoke (although I do make good coffee, too). Jacques's role was to feed us (too much) and to tell us that we were all wrong. The cats were very supportive, most of the time.

My grandmother died without seeing me married. Father Ambrosie's gone too, fishing from some cloud in heaven and drinking some local wine. As for me, I'm still waiting for Hollywood to return my phone calls and taking regular doses of Annie's verbal therapy, while Mr. Coby is trying to stop smoking (unsuccessfully so far).

If you don't believe me, come over for dinner and see for yourself. Just bring your cube—we have everything else.

—*Slobodan D. Pešić*

ABOUT THE AUTHORS

Annie Gottlieb is a freelance writer specializing in psychology. She has contributed to many publications, including *Mirabella, McCall's,* and the *New York Times* Book Review and Op-Ed page. She is the author of *Do You Believe in Magic?: Bringing the Sixties Back Home* and coauthor of *Wishcraft: How to Get What You Really Want.*

Slobodan D. Pešić is a director who has won awards all over the world for his film and television dramas. His first feature, "The Harms Case," debuted at Cannes and has garnered praise at film festivals in Berlin, Mannheim, Belgrade, Jerusalem, Montreal, Toronto, San Francisco, Chicago, and Hong Kong. He is at work on an American comedy, "Heart of a Dog."